SONGS OF FREEDOM:
The Psalter As A School of Prayer

by
Charles Cummings

Suiter Ann Josephine, c.s.c.
St. Mary's 1986
Augusta 4

Dimension Books, Inc.
Denville, New Jersey 07834

Dedication:

To all who are coming to birth in freedom.

Acknowledgements:

Grateful acknowledgement is made to The Grail, England, for permission to use *The Psalms: Singing Version* (Glasgow: William Collins Sons & Ltd., 1966).
Other scriptural quotations are taken from *The New American Bible,* copyright 1970, by the Confraternity of Christian Doctrine, Washington, D.C., with permission from copyright owner. All rights reserved.

ISBN 0-87193-245-8

Published by Dimension Books, P.O. Box 811
Denville, New Jersey, 07834

CONTENTS

INTRODUCTION

The psalter was the prayer book of Jesus and the early Christian community. Before and since that time, the psalms have been a source of spiritual sustenance and strength for many others. We have concerns today that the psalmists did not have, nearly three millennia ago, and we do not expect their writings to speak directly to our current problems. Yet, the psalms do have a message that speaks to the human heart, a message of freedom. Freedom is another word for salvation, in the full sense of being liberated for a life of outgoing love.

There are numerous commentaries on the psalter, psalm by psalm. There are excellent introductions to the psalter based on form-critical methods developed by modern biblical scholars. The spiritual riches of the psalter are not fully explored by these valuable studies, although no one who deals with the psalms overlooks their personal religious meanings, since the psalms speak to God more than about God. The present study examines a particular spiritual theme in the psalter, without attempting to say the final word even about that particular theme.

The psalter is a book to be prayed, not simply discussed or analyzed. By praying the psalms, we discover them as a school of prayer. By praying them, we learn about ourselves and about God. The psalmists' words express our need for liberation even where the bonds that are holding us may not be immediately perceived. Into the actual situation of our life, these powerful prayers summon the liberating God, who made a way for his people out of Egypt in the archetypal liberation-event of the exodus.

With the help of the psalmists we will explore the correlation between growth in prayer and growth in personal freedom. Deep prayer is a liberating experience because true freedom comes from an encounter with the merciful love of God. For God, to love is to save his servants and set them free to be his friends and share the divine life. "He brought me forth into freedom, he saved me because he loved me" (Ps 18:20). What it means to live in freedom can be seen best in the story of Jesus who was a perfect and totally free human being. Jesus lived the spirit of the psalms; they were his prayers to God his Father for the liberation of the world. The psalter opens for us the mystery of Christ and the mystery of the liberating love of God.

We are fortunate to live at a time when we have a variety of English translations of the psalter to choose from, all based on the Hebrew text. The Grail Psalter, which was approved for Catholic liturgical use in 1963, has been selected for quotation in this study. The reflections gathered in this book flow from years of living personally with the psalms in study and in daily prayer. I have found the songs of the psalter to be an exciting way to celebrate what St. Paul called "the freedom we enjoy in Christ Jesus" (Gal 2:4).

CHAPTER ONE

PSALMS AS STEADFAST FRIENDS

The psalter is a jewel set in the center of the Hebrew Bible, reflecting the turnings and fluctuations of Hebrew history. Yet the message of the psalms is for all people. These 150 inspired lyrics come from basic human experience and have been found to speak meaningfully to human beings of every faith, culture, century and education. The psalms are the heritage of all humanity.

The psalms speak with a universal voice because they rise from typical human situations. For example, the author of Psalm 18 was assailed by adverse circumstances and eventually turned to God: "In my anguish I called to the Lord; I cried to my God for help" (18:7). God heard the cry and came to the rescue at the moment when it seemed that the psalmist was going under: "He drew me forth from the mighty waters; he snatched me from my powerful foe, from my enemies whose strength I could not match" (18:17-18). Need for help from a stronger hand is the typical human experience that the psalmist expressed here, through the image of a drowning swimmer or a victim hounded by a powerful enemy. In this hopeless situation, God acted as savior setting the psalmist free: "He brought me forth into freedom, he saved me because he loved me" (18:20). The movement of the psalm is from distress to prayer to freedom as the psalmist's prayer was answered by a liberating God.

The psalms are songs of freedom because they replay this basic theme on nearly every page, with a thousand variations. In the process, the psalter has much to teach about prayer, about God, about human nature, and about freedom. Encounters with the God of salvation can be liberating. The psalms teach the dynamics of that encounter which is the heart of prayer, and therefore the psalter is a school of prayer. From the psalter we can learn how to pray in our own way, from where we are, without shame and without sham. The school of the psalter is far from dreary because the schoolmaster ultimately is God. For the psalmist, God is a constant, surprising presence, astonishingly eager to display his great wisdom and love.

In the school of the psalter we meet some of the fundamental questions affecting human effort, human suffering and loving, human living and dying. Because they address these perennial subjects, the psalms have great relevancy in every age including our own technological era. A Czech Communist philosopher, Milan Machovec, said in his book *A Marxist Looks At Jesus:* "Even an atheist can find that the Psalms are thoroughly 'up-to-date' and provide a dramatic description of what he is living through in the twentieth century." [1] In Latin America, the proponents of liberation theology pray the psalms with fresh insight into their message of deliverance from oppression. "The present experience of Latin American Christians is one that has been given profound expression in the psalms." [2] For average people in the richest or in the poorest countries of the world, the psalms find words to express the ordinariness of daily fidelity to duties, sustained by "lifting my eyes to the mountains from where shall come our help" (121:1). The psalms can be prayed every day for a lifetime without losing their interest because they continue to touch life in its experiences of growth, struggle, doubt, danger, joy. Wherever we are, a psalmist has been there before us.

A Christian Psalter?

Some Christians fail to find nourishment in the psalms because the name of Jesus Christ never occurs. What benefit, they wonder, can they draw from texts that propose models from the old covenant, like Abraham, Moses, and David instead of gospel models like Mary, the beloved disciple, and St. Paul? The psalms are populated by obscure figures like Phineas, Sihon, Amalek, Sisera. We have heard of names of places like Jerusalem, but we also meet references to Tarshish, Maribah, Mesech. The so-called cursing psalms seem to contradict the spirit of Jesus in the sermon on the mount. These objections culminate in an honest doubt about the usefulness of prayers from the Old Testament to nourish piety in the new covenant. Why do we not have psalms based on the gospel, that would sing of the works of Jesus and the lives of the first Christians?

Although there exists some Christian psalmody such as the Song of Zachary (Lk 1:68-79), the first Christians retained the collection of prayers they had used before accepting Jesus as savior and messiah. They felt no incongruity. The psalms were compatible with their faith in Christ, and may even have reinforced their faith because some of the psalms prophesied Christ. The risen Jesus said to his two disciples on the way to Emmaus, "Everything written about me in the law of Moses and the prophets and psalms had to be fulfilled" (Lk 24:44). In telling the parable of the tenants, Jesus implied that he was the stone of which Psalm 118:22 speaks: "The stone which the builders rejected has become the cornerstone. This is the work of the Lord, a marvel in our eyes" (Mt 21:42). On another occasion when Jesus was debating with the Pharisees about whose son the messiah was, he applied to himself a verse in Psalm 110: "How is it that David under the Spirit's influence calls him 'lord,' as he does: 'The Lord said to my lord, Sit at my right hand, until I humble your enemies beneath your feet' " (Mt 22:43-44). When some children in the temple shouted "Hosanna to the Son of David," Jesus thought of Psalm 8:3: "On the lips of children and of babes you have found praise" (Mt 21:15-16). As he hung dying on the cross, Jesus identified with the psalmists and repeated their words: "My God, my God, why have you forsaken me?" (Ps 22:2; Mt 27:46), and "Into your hands I commend my spirit" (Ps 30:6; Lk 23:46).

The evangelists quoted verses of the psalms to place the events of Christ's life in continuity with earlier records of sacred history. Matthew thought of a psalm when he wished to describe how Jesus taught in parables (Ps 78:2; Mt 13:34), as John did when describing the righteous zeal of Jesus for the temple (Ps 69:10; Jn 2:17), and when the soldiers who had crucified him cast lots for his robe (Ps 22:19; Jn 19:24). Of all the books in the Hebrew Bible, Psalms and Isaiah are quoted most by the authors of the New Testament.

Because many of the psalms could be re-read in a Christological sense and given a fuller meaning, there was no compelling need for the early church to compile a specifically Christian psalter. New Testament authors were satisfied to find messianic prophecies in the psalms. They could trace in the psalter and in the life of Christ the thread of a single, coherent story, the story of God's progressive revelation of his liberating love. The historical fact is that the Holy Spirit did not inspire a new psalter for Christians. We can conclude that a totally new psalter was unnecessary.

What is expected is that we learn to find in the psalter the word "that comes from the mouth of God" which we need to live on (Mt 4:4).

One effect of praying the Hebrew psalter is to survey the sequence of the history of salvation from the creation of heaven and earth to the call of Abraham, to the lifetime of Jesus, to the final age of the new creation. Again and again in the sweep of this arc, God intervened to liberate and save his people from some form of bondage. The coming of Christ was in one sense a completely fresh start, but in a larger context it was the repetition in definitive and unsurpassable form of liberation from bondage. The liberating acts of God our savior are repeated in large and small ways in the lives of his people down through the ages to our own day. The psalms intone this song of freedom and are perennially meaningful to Christians.

The Fuller Sense of the Psalms

If we do not have a Christian psalter, we have a psalter that has been Christianized by centuries of use and interpretation. The Fathers of the Church and the monks of the middle ages did not always know or feel bound by the literal sense of the psalms, and prayed them as if they applied in a fuller sense to the ministers and sacraments of the church, to the Virgin Mary and other saints, and even to ecclesiastical questions in their own day. St. Augustine, for example, interpreted Psalm 22 as if it had been composed with the fourth-century Donatist heretics in mind.

Today we will not be inclined to follow interpretations that seem strained and artificial, but we too can encounter Christ in the psalter. The psalms are the word of God, and we believe that the word of God became flesh in Jesus Christ (Jn 1:14). The fuller sense of the psalms is revealed in our dialogue with the word of God. The word of God is inexhaustibly efficacious and fruitful for the whole world. Through the prophet Isaiah, God said:

> Just as from the heavens the rain and snow come down and do not return there till they have watered the earth, making it fertile and fruitful, giving seed to him who sows and bread to him who eats, so shall my word be that goes forth from my mouth; it does not return to me void but shall do my will, achieving the end for which I sent it (Is 55:10-11).

In our dialogue with the word of God, we permit it to achieve the end—the fuller meaning and purpose— for which it was sent. Dialogue implies both listening to the words spoken to us, and making our own response. Sometimes we pray a psalm in the name of Christ who calls his disciples together and gathers them into the prayer he offers to God. Sometimes we pray the psalms in our own name as expressions of our need to ask for assistance or to rejoice in the nearness of God our savior. Either way, we pray with and through Christ who is the creative word of God ceaselessly at work to do God's will. Preaching to the Christian people in his cathedral at Hippo, St. Augustine found this way to express the fuller sense of the psalms:

> Let no one hearing the words of a psalm say, "This is not Christ praying," or again, "This is not myself praying." Rather let him be conscious that he is within Christ's body, and acknowledge both that "Christ is speaking" and that "I am speaking." You must not say anything without him, and he says nothing without you.[3]

Augustine's broad vision of prayer as a corporate experience helps us understand the psalms in their cultic, communitarian context. According to biblical scholars, most of the psalms originated to accompany liturgical worship in the temple or synagogue. Even psalms written in the first person singular and expressing the most personal sentiments towards God were intended to be used in a public context of sacred cult. The psalms do not support individualistic piety but draw from communal worship-experience to foster personal growth and intimacy with God.

The Song of the Word

The psalms emerged from a particular culture under particular historical circumstances over a period of six or seven centuries, but in their literal and fuller sense they transcend their origins. In the psalms we can hear a universal human voice praying, thanking, complaining, telling stories, sometimes cursing. The psalmists "express the pain and hope, misery and confidence of men of any age and land, and especially sing of faith in God, his revelation and his redemption."[4] The psalms teach us how to pray on behalf of human beings throughout the world who long in the depths of their hearts for peace and justice, for release from the routine of endless toil, for their share in the kingdom of God. Liberation is the implicit or explicit theme in many of the psalms.

The lyric prayers of the psalter are the song that the exiled Israelites refused to sing by the rivers of Babylon:

It was there that they asked us, our captors, for songs,
   our oppressors, for joy.
"Sing to us," they said, "one of Zion's songs."
   Oh, how could we sing the song of the Lord on alien soil?
(137:3-4)

The song of the Lord requires a human instrument to make its voice heard. The word of God sings life-giving songs through those who pray the psalms. A Christian writer of the third century, Clement of Alexandria, felt that these songs express the entire created universe in its longing for ultimate liberation. Clement wrote:

> The heavenly Word sings on the immortal throne the new harmony which is named after God, the new song. ... Bypassing the lyre and the zither which are instruments without soul, the Word harmonized, by means of the Holy Spirit, the world and man who is a microcosm of soul and body. The Word of God sings to the Father with this living instrument and accompanies his voice with his instrument which is man.[5]

For an English monk of the fourteenth century, Richard Rolle, the celestial song was not simply a metaphor but an entrancing song which he heard physically while praying the psalms. The experience was frequent, and it transformed his life of prayer, as we learn from numerous references in his writings. Here is his description of the initial experience:

> When I was sitting in that same chapel and I was singing the psalms in the evening before supper as well as I was able, I jumped as if at the ringing, or rather, the playing of stringed instruments, above me. And further, when I strained toward these heavenly sounds by praying with all my desire, I do not know how soon I experienced the blending of melodies within myself and drew forth the most delightful harmony from heaven, which remained with me in my spirit. For my meditation was continually transformed into the song of harmony, and it is as if I have odes in meditating. And further, I have enjoyed that same sound in psalmody and in the prayers themselves.[6]

In the Spirit

The psalms are the words of human beings like ourselves, but they were used as public prayers in the daily temple services and on special occasions such as the coronation of a king of Israel. In the course of time, the psalms were collected, divided into units, put in sequence, edited, and handed on to subsequent generations as part of Israel's sacred writings. They have been accepted as inspired word of God by Jews and Christians alike for more than two thousand years. We can say that the Spirit of God engendered these poems in the mind and heart of the human authors who found the words that corresponded to their interior inspiration.

As prayers addressed to God, the psalms have a privileged status because we believe they are words in which God desires prayer to be cast. What human being knows the kind of prayers that may please or displease God? "We do not know how to pray as we ought; but the Spirit himself makes intercession for us," says St. Paul, for "the Spirit intercedes for the saints as God himself wills" (Rom 8:26-27). Blaise Pascal put it this way: "Only God speaks well to God." God speaks in our language, expressing our own desires better than we ourselves. These ideas are implied when it is said that the psalms were written by God or written in the Spirit.

A contemporary Jewish author, Elie Wiesel, tells the story of an eighteenth century Rabbi, Levi-Yitzhak of Berditchev, who wanted to teach his people that the prayers they recited came from God. The entire congregation was gathered on the Day of Atonement, waiting for their leader to begin the final prayer so that they could break their lengthy fast. But the Rebbe waited for an hour, and then another hour, until the people's impatience turned to anguish. At last the Rebbe began to speak, and he told the congregation that there was someone in their midst who wanted to pray but felt too unskilled to find the right words to address to God. Instead he exposed the fears of his heart and said:

> You are God; I am but a man. You are Almighty and know everything; I am weak and ignorant. All I can do is decipher the twenty-two letters of the sacred tongue; let me give them to You to make into prayers for me and they will be more beautiful than mine.[7]

Rebbe Levi-Yitzhak raised his voice to draw the concluding lesson: "And that, brethren, is why we had to wait. God was busy writing."

It is because the psalms were written or engendered by the Spirit of God that they can be a school of prayer for those who are willing to be students. "The Spirit scrutinizes all matters, even the deep things of God" (1 Cor 2:10). The same Holy Spirit who originally inspired the psalmist's words keeps them living and pregnant with fresh meanings waiting to be born in the heart of one who prays with openness and receptivity. Written in the Spirit, the psalms are most fruitfully prayed in the spirit. The psalms resonate deeply in hearts that are in harmony with the Spirit of God, attentive and receptive to the Spirit rather than to the flesh. St. Paul reminded the Romans: "You are not in the flesh; you are in the spirit, since the Spirit of God dwells in you" (Rom 8:9).

The psalms have a spiritual potency to nourish us interiorly, in the spirit, with their life-enhancing, liberating message. Through repetition of the basic themes of praise, thanksgiving, repentance, and pleas for salvation, the psalms are a pedagogue of prayer, guiding, instructing, offering examples. It is the role of the Holy Spirit to "instruct us in everything" (Jn 14:26), and to "guide us to all truth" (Jn 16:13). As the Paraclete who is "with us always" (Jn 14:16), the Holy Spirit bears witness to us that "this God of ours is a God who saves" (Ps 68:21), "who makes safe the path of one he loves" (Ps 37:23), and who "leads the prisoners forth into freedom" (Ps 68:7). Indeed, "where the Spirit of the Lord is, there is freedom" (2 Cor 3:17).

Discussing the spiritual potency of the psalter, Cistercian Abbot Andre Louf writes: "As our outward man decreases from day to day while our inner man grows, so the letter of the psalm too falls away like a shell that becomes superfluous, whereas the essential content of *Pneuma,* the spiritual potency of the psalm, is more and more plainly felt."[8] As the psalms are prayed in the spirit, a certain reversal of order may take place between outward and inward. The words of the psalm spring from a deep source within, as if rising from the speaker's own spirit instead of being read from a book or given out from memory.

One of the earliest descriptions of this experience can be found in the conferences of the desert fathers recorded by John Cassian in the fifth century. Cassian and his friend, Germanus, visited Abba Isaac in the Egyptian desert and questioned him about prayer. In his second conference, Abba Isaac spoke of praying psalms when the psalm "is not like something committed to memory but like something implanted into our very nature which we bring to birth from the deep desires of the heart."[9] What has taken place is a personalization or assimilation of the essential content of the psalms, so that the speaker prays them "not as composi-

tions of the biblical author but as originating from himself
as prayers springing from the depths of his own contrite
heart." Abba Isaac went on to explain how it is possible to
put ourselves in the psalmist's place as author because we
share the same spiritual experience:

> If we have the same desires of heart as expressed in any
> sung or read psalm, we become like its author and are able
> to anticipate rather than follow its meaning. In other words,
> sensing the drift of the words before we know them, our
> memory triggers a recollection of something that happened
> to us or is happening in daily life. As we sing, we are refer-
> ring to something our carelessness has brought on, or our
> earnestness has achieved, or divine providence has arranged,
> or the temptation of Satan has deceived us with, or forget-
> fulness has lost for us, or human weakness has yielded to, or
> sheer ignorance has brought about. All these emotions we
> find expressed in the psalms so that we might recognize what
> is happening to us by looking in the psalter as into a perfect-
> ly clear mirror, where we discover our own experiences
> reflected back to us rather than hear about the experiences
> of someone else.

It was the teaching of these early spiritual masters that the
psalms can lead to the deepest personal experience of the
word of God. The history of salvation and liberation
celebrated in the psalter is the pattern of our own personal
liberation and sanctification. God's ways of encountering
his people are constant through the centuries, and our own
basic religious aspirations are reflected in the book of
psalms. Writing in the twelfth century, William of St.
Thierry said to Carthusians who used the psalter daily:
"You will never understand David [i.e. the psalmist] until
by experiencing you have made the very sentiments of the
psalms your own."[10]

Who Prays the Psalms?

The psalter, like all sacred scripture, belongs to everyone. Everyone has a right to take advantage of this treasury, and enjoy it at any time. Not every psalm or every verse in each psalm will be equally inspiring and illuminating, but there is variety enough in these 150 songs to respond to almost anyone's need and mood. Jews and Christians have lived intimately with the psalms for more than two millennia. Some examples from Christian history may be encouraging.

Jesus prayed the psalms. He is "that marvelous chanter of psalms," in St. Augustine's felicitous phrase. The occasional references to particular verses in the psalter are evidence of Jesus' familiarity with these prayers. He would have heard the psalms used in the synagogue service that he attended every sabbath in his town of Nazareth. It is likely that he knew some of the psalms by heart, since memorization of sacred texts was a common practice. His own teaching during his public ministry was imbued with the major themes of the psalter, especially trust and dependence on God. Jesus, who was both the Word of God and a human being like us in all things "except sin" (Heb 4:15), prayed often to his Father in solitude, but we have no way of knowing to what degree the psalter was his own school of prayer for these periods of closer communion with his father.

In the years following the death and exaltation of Jesus, the early Christian community accepted gentile converts and eventually separated itself from Jewish liturgical services in order to worship and break bread together in remembrance of Jesus. Several texts in the New Testament suggest that these Christians took the psalter with them, in Hebrew or in Greek, and later in Latin. The *Book of Acts* tells how the

eleven apostles stayed in an upstairs room in Jerusalem after
the ascension of Jesus. Some women met with them including "Mary the mother of Jesus, and his brothers."
Without explicit reference to psalms, we are told that "they
devoted themselves to constant prayer" (Ac 1:14). Immediately afterwards we are told that they decided to choose
a successor to Judas, since Peter had noted that, "It is written in the book of Psalms, 'Let his encampment be desolate;
may no one dwell on it' [Ps 69:26], and again, 'May another
take his office' [Ps 109:8]" (Ac 1:20). In other writings, the
letter of James says, "If a person is in good spirits, he
should sing a hymn of praise" (Jas 5:13, literally "sing a
psalm", as also in 1 Cor 14:15). And the Colossians are exhorted: "Sing gratefully to God from your hearts in psalms,
hymns, and inspired songs" (Col 3:16, as also in Eph 5:19).
The custom had begun.

A single anecdote from the monastic tradition of fourth-
century Egypt will be sufficient to show why the psalter remained a preferred form of Christian prayer. St. Macarius
the Great was an anchorite of great holiness, but others in
the desert surpassed him in prayerfulness. There were two
brothers who had learned from Macarius himself how to
live as monks, keeping silence, weaving baskets from reeds,
praying the psalms together at specified intervals. Macarius
visited them after three years to check their progress. In the
early morning, all of them recited the customary twelve
psalms. "The younger brother chanted five psalms in
groups of six verses and an alleluia, and at each verse a
tongue of flame came out of his mouth and ascended to
heaven. Likewise with the elder, when he opened his mouth
to chant, it was like a column of fire which came forth and
ascended up to heaven."[11] In that way Macarius learned

that the elder brother was already a perfect man, but the demons were still tempting the younger. The fire that left their mouth when they prayed symbolized the fervor and devotion with which they recited the psalms. The younger was like a small tongue of flame, the elder like a column of fire rising from a completely purified heart. The story concludes by saying that the elder brother died a few days later, and the younger a few days after that.

The Latin psalter was still understood and loved during the medieval period of church history. A Belgian Cistercian nun of the early thirteenth century, Beatrice of Nazareth, is said by her biographer to have been able to recite the psalter by heart, without fault and in the right order, at age five. Such biographies need to be interpreted critically, but there may have been a partial basis for this report. A Flemish mystic of about the same period, St. Lutgard, is said to have prayed for the grace of understanding the psalter at real depth. Her request was granted, but after some time she made a further request to the Lord Jesus, asking with complete freedom and artlessness, "I want your heart." The psalter had done its work as a school of prayer, leading Lutgard to a stage of perfect love.

The religious rules under which thousands of men and women have lived throughout the Christian centuries prescribe recitation of the psalms as a daily practice. The formative influence of these psalms, repeated again and again with their unique outlook on the human condition and on God, cannot be overestimated. The official prayer of the Roman Church, called the Liturgy of the Hours, is recited daily by all the clergy and includes psalms in each of its sections. The texts of the Eucharistic liturgy use verses of the psalms plentifully. The lectionary provides an appropriate psalm as a response to the first reading at the Eucharist. For many Christians, those verses after the reading are their only exposure to the psalms.

Some, however, have discovered that the psalter is not solely for public use and not solely for priests and religious. The psalms have been discovered as personal prayers or the starting point of personal prayer by a variety of people who are seeking to live and love more deeply and freely. There are even people who know one or more of the psalms by heart, such as the comforting Psalm 23 "The Lord is my shepherd", and who find that verses recited from memory evoke a peaceful region within them. Someone who treasured the psalms all her life was Dorothy Day, the founder of the Catholic Worker movement. Years before her conversion to Catholicism, when she was imprisoned briefly, she asked for a Bible and found great consolation and strength in reading the psalms. In her prison cell, she may have resonated particularly with the theme of freedom in the psalter. Although Dorothy Day did not write or speak much about prayer, her friends say that she had a genuine spirit of prayer especially in the final years before her death in 1980. She began each day with the psalms that were her favorites. Those who brought her breakfast and medicine in the early morning would find her propped up in bed, her silvery white hair braided and the braid pinned over the top of her head like a coronet, with the book of psalms open on her lap and a cup of coffee in her hand. Dorothy Day was not under obligation to recite the psalms but did so out of love, because they expressed her own vital need for praise, thanksgiving, supplication and repentance. A woman who dedicated her life to serving the poor found daily renewal in these songs of freedom.

Another example shows the psalms bringing strength and comfort to a woman as she died from cancer. Michele Murray was a poet, novelist, literary critic, and a convert from Judaism to Catholicism. She met death with full awareness and deliberate preparation, at the age of forty. Her final hours were spent at home with her husband. At her request, he played the Mozart records that were her favorites. Then she asked him to read to her the psalms she had first heard and loved in her childhood. In this gentle way, Michele Murray handed her life back into her Creator's hands.

American evangelist, Dr. Billy Graham, has told of his personal practice of daily contact with the psalter, even in his busy schedule of travel, Bible study, television appearances, and personal counseling. He has found in this literature a constant source of inspiration and strength. As he described it: "For many years I have made it a practice to read five Psalms and a chapter of the book of Proverbs each day, aside from my other Bible reading and study, and it has been a great blessing to me."[12] For Graham, the proverbs are words of wisdom for dealing with one's neighbor graciously and justly, but the psalms focus more directly on personal relationship with God. It is because of this transparent orientation to God that people of every age and status are drawn to the psalter again and again. For, as Thomas Merton has noted:

> The function of the psalms is to reveal to us God as the "treasure" whom we love because he has first loved us, and to hide us, heart and soul, in the depths of his infinite light. The Psalms, therefore, lead us to contemplation.[13]

NOTES

1. Milan Machovec, *A Marxist Looks at Jesus* (Philadelphia: Fortress Press, 1976), p. 29.
2. Gustavo Gutierrez, *We Drink From Our Own Wells: The Spiritual Journey of a People* (Maryknoll, New York: Orbis Books, 1984), p. 19.
3. St. Augustine, *Sermon On Psalm 85:1,* trans. in Maria Boulding, *Prayer: Our Journey Home* (Ann Arbor: Servant Books, 1979), p. 50.
4. *General Instruction on the Liturgy of the Hours* (1983), No. 107, United States Catholic Conference Publishing Service, #898.
5. Clement of Alexandria as quoted in *Consecrated Life* Vol. 3, No. 1, pp. 81-82.
6. Richard Rolle, *The Fire of Love* (Garden City: Image Books, 1981), p. 148.
7. Elie Wiesel, *Souls On Fire* (New York: Random House, 1973), p. 109.
8. Andre Louf, *Teach Us To Pray* (Chicago: Franciscan Herald Press, 1975), p. 56.
9. John Cassian, *Conference* X:11, J.P. Migne, PL 49, author's translation. The next two quotations are from the same place.
10. William of St. Thierry, *Golden Epistle,* trans. Theodore Berkeley, *Cistercian Fathers* 12 (Kalamazoo, Michigan: Cistercian Publications, 1980), p. 51, No. 121.
11. *Sayings of the Desert Fathers, Alphabetical Collection,* trans. Benedicta Ward (Kalamazoo, Michigan: Cistercian Publications 1975), p. 114, No. 33.
12. Billy Graham in Foreword to *Words of Wisdom from Living Psalms and Proverbs* paraphrased by Kenneth Taylor, compiled by George Wilson (Wheaton, Illinois: Tyndale House, 1967), p. 7.
13. Thomas Merton, *Bread In The Wilderness* (New York: New Directions, 1953), p. 8.

CHAPTER TWO

THE POETRY OF THE PSALMS

This book proposes the theme of freedom as a key to the spiritual riches of the psalter. Before exploring this theme in detail, it will be helpful to have an overview of the psalter according to its literary and poetic form. Modern study of the psalms according to principles of scientific biblical exegesis has revealed that the Israelite psalmists expressed their personal message in forms that were common to the literary culture of the Near East. Poetry analogous to the psalms in content and form has been discovered in Babylon, Ugarit, Nineveh, and in Egypt.

The psalmists, who celebrated their God-given freedom, retained that freedom in their use of poetic forms. A particular psalm might shift from one mood or theme to another, making classification difficult. For that reason, among others, there is not always universal agreement on how to classify the 150 psalms, nor even on the categories themselves.[1] For our purposes it will be enough to survey three principal literary types that will describe most of the psalms, and to make brief mention of several minor categories, such as the so-called cursing psalms.

Psalms of Praise

These songs or hymns begin with an invitation to praise God, or an acclamation such as, "How great is your name, O Lord our God, through all the earth!" (8:1). They go on to tell why God should be praised: because of who God is and what he has done through his creative power and saving love, how he has intervened in Israel's history. Psalms of praise may conclude by repeating the acclamation of the opening verse or by some new formula of blessing and praise that sums up the mood of the psalm.

The final psalm in the psalter is a song of praise that lifts this theme to its highest register, concluding with a universal invitation: "Let everything that lives and breathes give praise to the Lord, Alleluia" (150:6). Psalms in this category often call on musical instruments to help generate a tone of enthusiasm, joyfulness, newness, playfulness. In this family are some of the "Hallel" psalms—113, 135-136, 145-150—named from the acclamation "Alleluia" found at the beginning or end of the psalm and meaning "Praise Yah [Yahweh]". Also included in this family are psalms 8, 19, 29, 33, 96, 104, 111, 114, 117.

To consider one example, it is typical of psalms of praise to call upon all creation to join the act of worship being offered to God. The psalmist summons sea creatures, oceans, fire and hail, snow and mist, mountains and hills, fruit trees and cedars, beasts wild and tame, sun and moon and shining stars. Like the conductor of an orchestra, the psalmist directs a cosmic symphony of praise:

> Shout to the Lord all the earth, ring out your joy . . .
> Let the sea and all within it thunder;
>   the world and all its peoples.
> Let the rivers clap their hands, and the hills ring out their joy
>   at the presence of the Lord:
>   for he comes, he comes to rule the earth (98:4, 7-9).

A Christian praying this psalm today gives a voice to mute creatures that glorify God simply by being themselves and following the laws of their existence. In the theology of St.

Paul, there is a bondedness between ourselves and the whole created world which eagerly awaits its share "in the glorious freedom of the children of God" (Rom 8:21). As we use the psalms of praise, we perform a priestly, liturgical function on behalf of the non-human environment, drawing it closer to the new creation, closer to the Creator of all beings, closer to the fullness of the risen Christ.

Perhaps even more important, the psalms of praise call us to give a voice to our fellow human beings throughout the world whose own free worship of God has been silenced by ignorance, doubt, or circumstances beyond their control. In their name also, and on their behalf, we sing praise—on behalf of "all earth's kings and peoples, earth's princes and rulers, young men and maidens, old men together with children" (148:11-12). We gather together all these subjects, human and non-human, and give them our voice to praise and glorify God. As we use the psalms of praise, all heaven and earth move slightly closer to fulfillment, completion, and wholeness because of their solidarity with us in a cosmic endeavor.

Psalms of Petition

This family includes more than a third of the psalter, and it is here especially that the theme of liberation and salvation emerges. Petitions are made by the collective community or by an individual who may be a corporate "I" or an individual "I". Included in this group, among many others, are psalms 3, 51, 64, 86, 142, 143.

In the typical structure, the psalmist calls out to God for help, often invoking the personal name of God, Elohim or Yahweh. The use of the sacred name is already a powerful prayer of petition in itself, like a child crying for help with the single word "Mama". After this opening, the psalmist goes into detail about his or her predicament and begs for help. Because of the vivid description of afflictions—sickness, persecution by enemies, spiritual trials, the approach of death—these psalms are also called laments. Psalms of petition often end with an expression of confidence that the prayer has been heard, or will surely be heard now, and so the psalmist gives thanks and praise for deliverance.

"This is my prayer to you, my prayer for your favor. In your great love, answer me, O God, with your help that never fails" (69:14). Such cries for help can be said as easily by us today as when they were expressed for the first time centuries ago. "A pure heart create for me, O God, put a steadfast spirit within me. Do not cast me away from your presence, nor deprive me of your holy spirit" (51:12-13). These psalms speak to the perennial mystery of physical and spiritual suffering in human life, when God no longer seems near or powerful. Affliction is one of the most effective means of testing and purifying our faith in God. Affliction can make us surrender to God almost more quickly than anything else, or can drive us to the edge of despair. Affliction that we cannot do anything about except pray for relief can teach us how far God is beyond our control or manipulation, and how totally we depend on God's favor like the poor depend on a benefactor for their survival:

> You have burdened me with bitter troubles
>   but you will give me back my life.
> You will raise me from the depths of the earth;
>   You will exalt me and console me again.
> So I will give you thanks on the lyre
>   for your faithful love, my God (71:20-22).

The psalms did not reach the explanation of suffering that we find in the New Testament, but already in verses such as these there is a suggestion of a mystery of death and resurrection that was fulfilled in a transcendent way by Jesus Christ. Psalm 22, the passion psalm, belongs to this group and was prayed at least in part by Christ on the cross, as he offered the price of definitive human liberation. This group of psalms expressed and sustained Christ's own trust and love during his passover from death to exaltation. The voice of the afflicted one crying out in these psalms is the voice of Christ, and of all who dwell in the world of suffering.

Psalms of Thanks

"O give thanks to the Lord for he is good; for his love endures forever" (107:1). The psalms in this family begin with some expression of gratitude like this. God has heard the psalmist's petition, and the response is grateful praise. Some of the psalms included in this class are 23, 30, 40, 41, 92, 103, 116, 138.

Psalms of thanks are close to the psalms of praise in their structure. There is more emphasis on thanks for a particular favor received in the midst of distress. God is given credit as the savior. Here also the theme of liberation is prominent. These psalms acquired a somewhat formal style from frequent use in the temple liturgy, to accompany a sacrifice of thanksgiving. As the worshipper offered an animal victim and baked goods, he or she might have said: "I will sacrifice to you with willing heart and praise your name for it is good; for you have rescued me from all my distress and my eyes have seen the downfall of my foes" (58:8-9).

Someone who had recovered from an almost mortal illness or had been saved from some catastrophe would feel

drawn to the temple of the Lord to "take my place around
your altar, singing a song of thanksgiving, proclaiming all
your wonders" (26:6-9). The experience of God's saving
power is like a resurrection to new life, and the psalmist
burst into jubilant thanks, realizing that he or she has
passed "from prison to the open spaces, from weeping to
laughter, from sorrowful complaint to gay dances, from
sackcloth to wedding garments, from the gates of death to
the gates of the daughter of Zion."[2]

The Fathers of the Church considered Psalm 118 as the
easter song of thanks on the lips of the risen Christ. The
concluding verse says: "You are my God, I thank you; my
God, I praise you. Give thanks to the Lord for he is good;
for his love endures forever" (118:28-29). Jesus is the
thankful one par excellence, the one who offers perpetual
Eucharist. The gospel of Matthew describes one exclamation of praise and thanks: "On one occasion Jesus spoke
thus: 'Father, Lord of heaven and earth, to you I offer
praise [I thank you]; for what you have hidden from the
learned and the clever you have revealed to the merest
children" (Mt 11:25).

Disciples of Jesus can share that spirit of gratitude,
because we have received the revelation Jesus spoke of, the
revelation of a God who loves and liberates. The psalms in
this category come easily to grateful hearts: "O God, we
ponder your love within your temple! Your praise, O God,
like your name reaches the ends of the earth" (48:10-11).
The more we perceive everything as gift, as proof of God's
loving providence, the more easily we live the spirit of these
psalms of thanks.

Additional Groupings

Besides the three principal families, there are several other sub-groups that may be noted briefly. Not all these divisions represent true literary forms with a distinct structure, but they are grouped together by content or dominant theme.

The *royal psalms,* such as Psalms 2, 45, 110, allude to a king. These three came to be understood in a messianic sense, because the messiah, whose name means "anointed one", was expected to be a savior-king. Psalm 110 is the psalm most frequently quoted in the New Testament: "The Lord said to my Lord: 'Sit at my right hand' " (110:1). Psalms that refer to the king's throne—Psalms 47, 93, 96-99—are sometimes called enthronement psalms.

The *wisdom psalms* are didactic and reflective, teaching about the law and the duties of an upright person. The first psalm in the psalter holds out the ideal of joyful fidelity to the law or will of God. Some wisdom psalms are alphabetical in structure, matching opening words to the letters of the alphabet. For example, there is the lengthy Psalm 119 which celebrates in 176 verses the law as sacrament of God's presence among his people.

There are *historical psalms,* such as Psalm 78 that recalls the plagues of Egypt and the exodus, or Psalm 106 that recounts the forty years of wandering in the desert. Remembering God's great acts of national liberation in the past is the basis for hope in new interventions.

Frequently used in the official daily prayer of the Roman Church are the *pilgrim psalms.* Originally these may have been sung during the three annual visits to the temple in Jerusalem, as the pilgrims climbed the hill to Zion. Fourteen psalms, psalms 120-134, have the Hebrew title "a song of ascents." St. Augustine called these the psalms of our journey to the heavenly Jerusalem.

Several psalms have been called *cursing psalms* because of their virulent emotion and their calls for vengeance on various named and unnamed enemies. Besides psalms 69, 83, 109, there are scattered verses in other psalms that express strong resentment and pray for divine judgment against persecutors. The psalmists made no effort to hide their emotions, whether of rage or of joy. They reacted to evil like someone who has hit his thumb with a hammer. The cursing psalms may cause some embarrassment to people who pray them today. It can be admitted that they come from a pre-Christian, even primitive, level of development. At the same time we might acknowledge the persistence of those same primitive elements in our own hearts, and in evil around us. The psalmists' curses could be transposed into protests against our own sinful inclinations and against the unjust structures in contemporary society.

Psalms as Songs

Understanding something about the principal families or literary forms that we find in the psalter can be a help in attuning us to the dominant mood of a particular psalm. The art form of the psalms is musical as well as literary. The title of the Book of Psalms in the Hebrew Bible, *tehillim*, means songs of praise. The Greek term, *psalmos*, from which our word "psalm" is derived means a song to be sung to the sound of a harp or similar stringed instrument.

The psalms were composed to be sung or at least spoken aloud. Something is lost when they are recited silently, or even privately rather than in a communal context. The shortest psalm in the psalter runs:

> O praise the Lord, all you nations,
>   acclaim him, all you peoples!
> Strong is his love for us;
>   he is faithful forever! (117:1-2)

The plural form and the bouyant, exultant spirit of this short song almost demand rendition by a chorus with instrumental accompaniment. Not all the psalms lend themselves so easily to singing, but they have musical rhythm in their poetic form. The rhythm would be most evident in the original Hebrew language, but it comes through occasionally in careful translations. In the second verse of Psalm 117, "strong is his love for us," the triple accent rhythm of the original is still evident, and that rhythm is frequent in the psalms.

A distinctive feature of the psalms as an art form is the use of parallelism—repeating the same thought in different words. The original Hebrew parallelism is usually preserved rather well in translation, as in the first verse of Psalm 117 above, where the second half repeats the meaning of the first:

> O praise the Lord, all you nations
>   acclaim him, all you peoples!

Poetic parallelism is often an aid to interpretation, and helps expand the vocabulary of liberation in the psalter by offering alternative images and phrases. Parallelism even enhances the prayerfulness of the psalms by slowing down the movement of thought, to allow the imagery to sink deeper into the heart and evoke a response from the whole person. The psalmist leads our hearts, minds and feelings back over the same theme again and perhaps again, in a circular pattern that frustrates logical progression but fosters contemplative presence.

Someone who uses the psalms for prayer is influenced both by their literary content and by their poetic form. The word of God in the psalms is encountered not merely on the literal, rational level but also on a non-rational, experiential level. The psalms communicate by what they say and how they say it. In this study we will be focusing on thematic content, but equally important, and perhaps more important for the relationship of prayer, is the rhythmic poetic form that resonates with unspoken longings of the heart. A French archbishop and theologian, Gabriel Garrone, has said: "In the chanting of the psalms there is an undeniable religious dynamism, a power of recollection that is to some extent independent of the intelligible content of the text."[3]

In the guidelines published by Rome for the General Instruction of the Liturgy of the Hours [1983], we are told: "Whilst certainly offering a text to our mind, the psalm is more concerned with moving the spirits of those singing and listening, and indeed of those accompanying it with music" (No. 103). The spirit can be moved and the heart lifted to God powerfully by non-rational means. We can be open and receptive to this dimension by responding to the spirit of music and poetry that runs through the psalter.

O sing a new song to the Lord, sing to the Lord all the earth.
   O sing to the Lord, bless his name! (96:1)

Sing a new song to the Lord, his praise in the assembly of
   the faithful.
   Let Israel rejoice in its maker,
   let Zion's sons exult in their king! (149:1).

If we become familiar with the psalms and allow them to filter down into the deeper, non-rational levels of our being, they have a way of coming back to us in snatches at other times or in other situations. Just as the melody of a catchy tune may pop into our mind at an odd moment and set us humming it, so a phrase from a psalm may return and animate us in a moment of dialogue with God. The memory soon passes, but there has been a spontaneous lifting of our mind and heart to God.

Anonymous Psalmist

Our present collection of 150 psalms was gathered over a period of six centuries or more. Some bear a title attributing them to King David. Modern biblical scholars would admit that at least a few of these—e.g. Psalm 18—may indeed go back to the Davidic monarchy and temple worship in the tenth century, but the original authors are unknown for the most part. The fact that the psalms can be classified in families, in spite of their diverse authorship and extended timespan, is due to the common religious faith and tradition that the authors shared. Behind these human authors we recognize the guiding inspiration of a single, holy spirit. To quote again from William of St. Thierry's letter to the Carthusians: "The Scriptures need to be read and understood in the same spirit in which they were written."[4]

Each of the psalmists had his or her own unique viewpoint, and none of them can speak for the entire book of psalms. In spite of their diverse approaches, we can pick up the strands of a unified outlook on the human condition in relation to the one, creating, liberating God. It is to this underlying convergence that we appeal when we trace a particular theme in the psalter, skipping from psalm to psalm and verse to verse. Because the authors are anonymous, the psalms come across virtually as the work of a single, inspired author expressing a broad range of moods and ideas. We may picture this author composing a collection of sacred songs to celebrate the freedom to be found in serving the one true Lord in his holy temple; the author passes on to others everything known about God's ways of dealing with the world.

As we grow in familiarity with the psalms, letting their message penetrate into our own consciousness, we gradually assimilate the psalmist's view of God, of the human condition, of the life of prayer. These, among others, are the living sources at which Jesus himself and the early Christians nourished their spirits. Because we bring to the psalter a highly developed Christian heritage and the discoveries of contemporary biblical scholarship, our reading of this body of sacred songs will be all the more fruitful. The anonymous Hebrew psalms become a school of Christian prayer and spirituality when we use them with faith and loving appreciation.

NOTES

1. The classification presented here is based principally on a study by Pius Drijvers, *The Psalms: Their Structure and Meaning* (New York: Herder & Herder, 1965). Although authors differ in classifying the psalms according to type, most depend directly or indirectly on the original work of the German scholar Hermann Gunkel.
2. Pius Drijvers, *The Psalms,* p. 93.
3. Mgr. Gabriel Garrone, *Psaumes et Priere*(Toulouse, 1952), p. 12, quoted by Albert Gelin, *Les Pauvres de Yahve* (Paris: Les Editions du Cerf, 1953), p. 112.
4. William of St. Thierry, *Golden Epistle,* trans. Theodore Berkeley, *Cistercian Fathers* 12 (Kalamazoo, Michigan: Cistercian Publications, 1980), p. 51, No. 121.

CHAPTER THREE

FROM BONDAGE TO FREEDOM

In order to understand the psalms as freedom songs, we need to highlight everything that belongs to this theme. In the process, other important themes recede into the background and are not discussed unless they relate to the topic of freedom. Placing a filter over the lens through which we view the psalms, we filter out the shades and tints of subjects that are more remote, so that the details of the experience of liberation will stand out more clearly. In this way we lay open the heart of the psalter as a record of God's life-giving, saving love.

Psalm 81 has God speak as savior, recalling his mighty act of liberating Israel from Egypt: "I freed your shoulder from the burden; your hands were freed from the load; you called in distress and I saved you" (81:7-8). In the Hebrew scriptures, the title of savior belongs by right to Yahweh, the God of Israel. "You are God my savior, in you I hope all day long because of your goodness, O Lord"(25:5-7). As savior of his people, God freed them from their bondage; salvation includes liberation.

One of the principal Hebrew words for salvation comes from the root *ysha* which means "to broaden, enlarge, make spacious." Liberation is implicit in this idea because the experience of being set free is the movement from a condition of bondage and constraint into a spaciousness where one can breathe deeply again. To be saved means to be delivered from confinement, oppression, narrow straits, tight bonds. To be saved is to be set free, set at large, set on a broad, open space with unhindered options in all directions. The desert into which God led his people after freeing them from Egypt was symbolic of their liberation—total spaciousness in which they were totally dependent on God for survival.

Paradigm of Liberation   *Luke 4:18-19 (Isaiah)*

God saves or sets his people free by throwing off the chains that bind them. The psalmists prayed to God their savior, beseeching him to intervene before it was too late. After he had liberated them, they gave thanks and celebrated their freedom with new songs of gladness. These basic steps—the affliction of the psalmist, the invocation of Yahweh, the experience of liberation, the culmination of gratitude—constitute a paradigm of liberation or salvation. The concrete description of each step varies according to particular circumstances, and may be implicit rather than explicit in a particular psalm, but the basic structure of a liberation-experience manifests itself in these four steps.

This paradigm of liberation is drawn from the psalms themselves. To look at an example where the different steps may be seen rather clearly, we may consider Psalm 40, especially its opening verses.

Ps. 40

2 I waited, I waited for the Lord and he stooped down to me;
   he heard my cry.
3 He drew me from the deadly pit, from the miry clay.
   He set my feet upon a rock and made my footsteps firm.
4 He put a new song into my mouth, praise of our God.

Here the psalmist looks back at the experience of being set free. In verse 2, he or she recalls waiting anxiously and crying to Yahweh for help. We are not told the nature of the affliction until verse 3; a description of the deadly pit and miry clay might have been part of the psalmist's original prayer for help. God's saving act of deliverance—the third and most central element—is recalled in expressive verbs: stooping down, drawing up, setting upon a rock, and giving the psalmist a firm footing. The result or effect of this dramatic rescue is the psalmist's new song of praise, and God is given credit for inspiring the psalm that thanks him. Verses 10 and 11 elaborate the content of the new song which was proclaimed in the great assembly of Israelites: "Your justice I have proclaimed, ... [and] your faithful help; I have not hidden your love and your truth." God's faithful help, literally, is "your salvation." The word *salvation* in any of its forms takes us back immediately to the root meaning of setting free. The psalmist has been drawn free from the clinging miry clay and given a firm stand on solid rock in a spacious place.

The psalmists, with their poetic creativity, often used language that depended on images and metaphors. We presume that language about miry clay and firm rock is metaphorical, even though a literal interpretation may be possible here and in many other places. The question would be hard to decide with certainty, and need not be a matter of anxiety since the ambiguity is fruitful. In the following example, from Psalm 18, the psalmist was liberated either from mighty waters described as powerful enemies, or from powerful enemies described as mighty waters. The poetic language gives us a general idea of the psalmist's predicament but not all the specifics.

The verses of Psalm 18 given below are selected to illustrate the four steps of the paradigm of liberation, minus the elaboration found in the intervening verses.

7 In my anguish I called to the Lord;
     I cried to my God for help.

17 From on high he reached down and seized me;
     he drew me forth from the mighty waters.

18 He snatched me from my powerful foe,
     from my enemies whose strength I could not match.

20 He brought me forth into freedom,
     he saved me because he loved me.

37 You gave me freedom for my steps;
     my feet have never slipped.

47 Praised be the God who saves me.

49 You saved me from my furious foes.
     You set me above my assailants.
     You saved me from violent men,

50 so I will praise you, Lord, among the nations:
     I will sing a psalm to your name.

The psalmist's anguish was due to mighty waters, powerful and furious foes that were wound around him like the ropes of death and the underworld. From this affliction—step one—the psalmist called upon the Lord for help. This desperate prayer—step two—roused God to action. The act of liberation is described in words that are explicit about freedom, a spacious place where the psalmist walks in security (verses 20, 37). Finally in step four, the psalmist sang a psalm of praise to God who has saved him (verses 47-50). That psalm of praise is Psalm 18 in its entirety. Occuring also in 2 Sm 22, this psalm is attributed to King David as a victory song after God had freed him from the hand of Saul and other enemies.

The basic structure of the Bible's songs of freedom is becoming clear after this consideration of Psalms 40 and 18. The four steps do not always occur in perfect, logical sequence, and one or another step might seem to be absent altogether, but knowledge of the complete paradigm often makes a psalm more intelligible. Not every psalm in the psalter follows the paradigm of the songs of freedom, but the paradigm remains a helpful key in many cases. An entire psalm can elaborate just one step of the paradigm; for example, step four can be expanded into an independent psalm of thanks or praise. The flexibility and range of these basic steps will be easier to appreciate as we examine each step in the following four sections.

Affliction

"The Bible," said the French scripture scholar Albert Gelin, "has given us a sampling of all human distress, in particular of religious distress and that of the mind."[1] In the psalms, the generic term for distress, *rhb*, connotes a cramped, constricting, narrow space, as if bound in a straitjacket. Distress is the polar opposite of freedom.

"I have no means of escape," cried the psalmist from the depths of distress (142:5). Sometimes the psalmist compared himself to a prisoner groaning in bondage and condemned to die. Prisoners were used for forced labor, a reminder of the years of slavery in Egypt when there was "a heavy burden on our backs" (66:11). There they were forced to carry baskets for Pharoah's construction projects.[2] In Psalm 81, God recalls how he liberated his people from slave labor: "I freed your shoulder from the burden; your hands were freed from the load. You called in distress and I saved you. ... I am the Lord your God, who brought you from the land of Egypt" (81:7, 8, 11).

Frequently, the psalmist's affliction came from enemies. He or she felt surrounded by them like "fierce bulls of

Bashan'' (22:13), encircled by "the jaws of these lions ...
the horns of these oxen" (22:22). The psalmist was no
match for their strength, for they were like raging beasts,
furious assailants pursuing relentlessly. They did not blush
at lying, perjury, slander, and the "treacherous tongue"
(120:3), because they had no fear of God and their "reward
is in this present life" (17:14). The wicked set traps, snares,
and pitfalls in the path of the innocent in order to trip them
up. It was God who helped the psalmists escape, as a bird
breaks free of the fowler's snare: "Indeed the snare has
been broken and we have escaped" (124:7).

Sometimes the psalmist complained of a generalized feeling of oppression, an interior terror matching the threat
from outside. "Relieve the anguish of my heart and set me
free from my distress. See my affliction and my toil, and
take all my sins away" (25: 17-18). Sin is thought to be the
deepest root of the feeling of depression, even if the faults
are hidden from the psalmist's awareness. "From hidden
faults acquit me; from presumption restrain your servant"
(19:13-14). The most insidious faults are those that present
no scandalous exterior symptoms: self-righteousness, self-
conteredness, and the presumption of uprightness.

Serious illness was another affliction that oppressed the
psalmists. Sickness narrows the invalid's world to the con-
fines of a "bed of pain" (41:4). If the sickness seems in-
curable, the invalid has the feeling of sinking deeper
towards death. Metaphors about being overwhelmed by
high waves occur in this context: "Do not let the deep
engulf me nor death close its mouth on me" (69:16). For the
Israelites, whose hope in personal immortality developed
only gradually, there was no distress like death and "the
anguish of the tomb" (116:3). If there were any savior from

disease and death, it would be Yahweh in his liberating love: "Your love to me has been great; you have saved me from the depths of the grave" (86:13).

The psalmists experienced affliction as threatening their foothold, the state of peace and security that they were accustomed to. Affliction came upon them as they walked nonchalantly in the presence of Yahweh. Prior to affliction is a condition of well-being when God is taken for granted as the one who is always present, always with his people. The people of God knew that they had only to call, and God would answer, "I am with you" (91:15). The history of God's fidelity to his covenant gave the Israelites this confidence. "God is for us a refuge and strength, a helper close at hand, in time of distress; so we shall not fear. ... The Lord of hosts is with us: the God of Jacob is our stronghold" (46:2, 4).

Affliction abruptly destroys this complacency. Whatever the precise cause of the affliction, the psalmist feels hemmed in on all sides with no one to help. Yahweh is inexplicably absent. All the negativity of the cosmos seems to assail the psalmist from within and without while God remains indifferent. Only at a later stage, in steps three and four, will the psalmist rediscover the nearness of God. At the moment, in the anxiety of affliction, the psalmist invokes Yahweh: "In my anguish I called to the Lord; I cried to my God for help" (18:7).

Invoking God's Help

The Hebrew term meaning "cry for help" is the same radical—*ysha*—that connotes salvation. Prayers for help and salvation are prayers for liberation. When the psalmist

For God to love is to save.[1]

called on God for help, the prayer was asking for divine intervention to set his servant free from affliction and restore the original condition of blessing and peace. God responds more to need than to eloquence, and even an uneloquent groan may be persuasive: "He looked down from heaven to the earth that he might hear the groans of the prisoners and free those condemned to die" (102:21). However, the poets who composed the psalms had no hesitation in using all their powers of eloquence to persuade God to look down from heaven and notice his servants' affliction.

Numerous psalms remind God that he is a savior who has helped his people repeatedly in the past. "This God of ours is a God who saves; the Lord our God holds the keys of death" (68:21). God is called rock of refuge, fortress, shield, mighty stronghold, king from of old, "giver of help through all the land" (74:12). He is asked to make known once more the saving power of his hand. The psalmist recalled the image of God as shepherd of Israel, carrying his people on his shoulder: "He brought forth his people like sheep; he guided his flock in the desert" (78:52). One of the psalmist's most frequent tactics is to touch God's heart by a disarming appeal to his mercy and love. "Help me, Lord my God; save me because of your love" (109:26). For God, to love is to save. God's mercy and care are shown by acts of saving help. God's justice also is manifest by setting his servants free from affliction, as Psalm 76:10 recalls: "God arose to judge, to save the humble of the earth."

In half a dozen psalms, God is implored to intervene for the sake of his name. God's personal name, Yahweh, may occur in these petitions—"For your name's sake, Lord, save my life" (143:11)—but God's name in the biblical sense is more than a personal designation. To invoke God's name is to invoke God's truth and holiness, his reputation as God of gods, the creator of heaven and earth (Gen 14:22; Is 43:10-11). The God of Israel is known as God by his saving acts. God's true name is revealed in the act of setting free.

In their prayers for God's help, the psalmists pursued still another line of approach. They called God's attention to themselves as his covenant partners. By reason of the covenant, they were his people and had a right to call on him for aid in distress. It was enough to assert that they were his people: "Save your people!" (28:9). It was enough, they hoped, for them to call on God and he would come because he was their God: "The Lord hears me whenever I call him" (4:4). "I called to the Lord in my distress; he answered and freed me" (118:5).

In case it might not be enough for God's people simply to cry out to the Lord, the psalmists reminded God that they were friends who had put their trust in him, a humble people whose spirit was crushed and whose heart was broken. They made him their refuge because they were helpless to save themselves: "The Lord protects the simple hearts: I was helpless so he saved me" (116:6). In simplicity, the afflicted psalmist protests that he or she is upright of heart, fearing God and keeping his law, one of the poor and lowly who thirsts for salvation, one who clings to God in love and belongs entirely to him—"Save me, for I am yours" (119:94). On these grounds, the psalmist is sure of God's love, but to make doubly sure reminds God of the piety of his mother, and for her sake begs mercy for himself: "Save your handmaid's son!" (86:16). If God is moved or amused by human oratory, there is much to notice here.

Being Set Free

The experience of being set free from affliction in response to a prayer for God's help is described in images that breathe of spaciousness and security. After the confinement of affliction, freedom comes like the flight of a bird in open space: "Our life, like a bird, has escaped!" (124:7). Freedom, we recall, has a metaphorical connection with the experience of moving from a constricted condition of bondage into a broad, open vista where every path is safe. "God leads the prisoners forth into freedom" (68:7).

In their description of being set free, the psalmists gave credit to God for leading them to level ground and making their feet stand firm. "You gave me freedom for my steps; my feet have never slipped" (18:37). Leading and guiding are phases of God's liberating activity. He will prevent his servant from stumbling, or from falling if he should happen to stumble: "The Lord guides the steps of a man and makes safe the path of one he loves. Though he stumble he shall never fall for the Lord holds him by the hand" (37:23-24).

The path marked out for the free person to walk is called the way of perfection or the path of life or the path of freedom. The one who walks it walks in truth, walks in the presence of God: "I will walk in the presence of the Lord in the land of the living" (116:9). Where does the path of freedom lead? Once, the path led out of slavery in the labor camp of Goshen, across the Sea of Reeds and the Sinai desert, to the mountain where God had chosen to dwell: "So he brought them to his holy land, to the mountain which his right hand had won" (78:54). Israel never forgot that experience of being set free and finding new life in the home prepared for the poor by God in his goodness (68:11).

The experience was repeated again after the Babylonian exile, at a time when some of the psalms were being written down and collected. The psalmists preferred concrete metaphors to abstract terms, but they came to realize that the path of freedom that they walked had its final destination not in a particular place but in the living presence of Yahweh their God. "You will show me the path of life, the fullness of joy in your presence" (16:11). The goal was to stand or to walk in the presence of Yahweh for evermore.

A further stage of insight was reached when the psalmists realized that they walked in the presence of God as long as they obeyed God's word and kept his law. The safe and level path was trust in God and fulfillment of his will: "Teach me to do your will for you, O Lord, are my God. Let your good spirit guide me in ways that are level and smooth" (143:10). Just as sin was understood to be the source of affliction in many cases, the source of inner freedom was understood to be fidelity to all the covenant obligations and commandments of God. Psalm 119 celebrates for 176 verses the psalmist's devotion to the law. "I will run the way of your commands; you give freedom to my heart" (119:32). To the experience of objective freedom from various forms of affliction, there corresponds a "freedom of heart", the interior freedom experienced by a heart in tune with the heart or will of God. The objective and subjective levels of freedom do not always coincide. The prisoner in chains may have freedom of heart, while one who walks free may be dragging interior chains around pitiably. The psalmist might be playing on both levels in any description of being set free.

Singing a Song of Thanksgiving

We come to the fourth and final stage in the paradigm of liberation. In response to an invocation made from extreme affliction, God rose up to set his servants free. " 'For the poor who are oppressed and the needy who groan I myself will arise,' says the Lord. 'I will grant them the salvation for which they thirst' " (12:6). Even at the darkest moments the psalmist had never quite given up all hope of rescue by God: "Why are you cast down, my soul, why groan within me? Hope in God; I will praise him still, my savior and my God" (42:12). Now, in the experience of once again standing free and secure in the presence of God, the psalmist gives full expression to feelings of gratefulness and joy of heart.

The liberated person is not content to seek out a hidden corner in order to give thanks privately. Yahweh's liberating love must be published far and wide. "I will tell of your name to my brethren and praise you where they are assembled" (22:23). The great liturgical assemblies of the tribes of Israel were privileged occasions for expressing thanks: "I will thank you in the great assembly, amid the throng I will praise you" (35:18). Even the foreign nations will be told of God's saving power and be invited to join in the universal song of thanksgiving.

The psalmist has a new song of praise to sing, inspired by God himself: "He put a new song into my mouth" (40:4). Or the new song is lovingly composed to fulfill a vow made when the psalmist was still groaning in bondage: "Bring my soul out of this prison and then I shall praise your name" (142:8). Many of the psalms of praise and thanksgiving may be taken as these new songs. Instrumental accompaniment increased the festal joy of these new songs: "So I will give you thanks on the lyre for your faithful love, my God. To you will I sing with the harp, to you the Holy One of Israel. When I sing to you my lips shall rejoice and my soul, which you have redeemed" (71:22-23). Hands that previously chapped at rough labor will now be used to "sound the timbrel, the sweet-sounding harp and the lute" (81:3), and to "raise the cup of salvation" (116:13) in the temple liturgy.

The psalmist whose heart rejoices in God's saving goodness plays the part of a cheerleader in summoning the people to song: "O come, ring out your joy, all you upright of heart!" (32:1). All are exhorted to be joyful in the Lord and to express themselves "with cries of deliverance" (32:7), shouting "God is great" (70:5), or "Lord, who is like you?" (35:10), as they rejoice in his liberation. It was in this way, with cries of joy and gladness, that God led his people out of Egypt on an unforgettable night of liberation: "He brought out his people with joy, his chosen ones with shouts of rejoicing" (105:43). Again and again, in their experience of affliction, the psalmists longed for a renewal of that saving act and that feeling of grateful joy: "O that Israel's salvation might come from Zion! When the Lord delivers his people from bondage, then Jacob will be glad and Israel rejoice" (14:7).

The concluding stage of thanksgiving is not a superfluous afterthought but an integral part of the total experience of liberation. Without this expression of thankful praise, the psalmist's new-found freedom would be imperfect from the start. To be set free is to move from oppression to a heart-expanding experience of God's saving love. If people feel free, they celebrate their freedom in some way that is as essential as song to a bird. The psalter provides no definitions of freedom, but we are close to the core when the psalmist says: "My soul shall be joyful in the Lord and rejoice in his salvation," remembering that salvation is another word for freedom (35:9). Another psalmist put it this way: "As for me, I trust in your merciful love; let my heart rejoice in your saving help" (13:6). Freedom means having a heart that rejoices in God its savior.

Liberation History

What we are calling the paradigm of liberation, with its four steps of affliction, invocation, setting free, and thanksgiving, is a pattern that the psalmists found repeated in Israel's history. Their own experience of being set free was felt to be in continuity with events of their nation's history, or else they were praying that events of the nation's past might be renewed for their benefit in the present. The psalmists saw themselves as parts of a larger, corporate personality constituted by the entire people of God; their personal histories found meaning in the great events of their people's past which were remembered, repeated, and carefully handed on to succeeding generations.

In the psalter we can discern past events of liberation that are evoked as grounds for hope in a new display of God's saving love. Psalm 126 seems to recall the return from captivity by the rivers of Babylon: "When the Lord delivered Zion from bondage, it seemed like a dream; then was our mouth filled with laughter, on our lips there were songs" (126:1-2). Psalm 144 looks back to the time when King David was rescued from the clutches of Saul and the Philistines: "You set David your servant free; you set him free from the evil sword; you rescued him from alien foes"

(144: 10-11). Developed at somewhat greater length is the precedent of the patriarch Joseph languishing in an Egyptian prison, his feet in chains, his neck bound with an iron collar. When Joseph's interpretation of the king's dream came true, he was liberated: "Then the king sent and released him; the ruler of the peoples set him free, making him master of his house and ruler of all he possessed" (105:20-21). All these examples are precedents for trusting Yahweh in the present affliction: "In you our fathers put their trust; they trusted and you set them free" (22:5).

Although the psalms recall these outstanding precedents, the primal event of liberation celebrated in the psalter is the exodus from Egypt. Israel was formed as the people of God by its experience of being set free from bondage in Egypt and led safely through the desert to the promised land. It is no exaggeration to say that the exodus was the counterpart of the creation of the world out of the darkness of chaos. Yahweh's victory over the Egyptian slavemasters as he led his people through the river dry-shod was the marvelous deed that brought forth a new creation, his chosen people: "So he brought out his people with joy, his chosen ones with shouts of rejoicing" (105:43).

The exodus was not only a sign of God's power—the invincible might of his strong hand and outstretched arm by which "he does whatever he wills" (115:3)—but also a sign of his liberating love. "For you, O God, are my stronghold, the God who shows me love" (59:10). God is the strong but gentle shepherd of Israel who led them to freedom in the fresh, green pastures of the promised land:

> Then he brought forth his people like sheep;
> he guided his flock in the desert.

He led them safely with nothing to fear,
  while the sea engulfed their foes.
So he brought them to his holy land,
  to the mountain which his right hand had won (78:52-54).

The four stages of the paradigm are evident in this experience of liberation.

The exodus was God's response to the cry of distress raised by the descendants of Abraham, Isaac and Jacob as they groaned under Pharaoh's yoke of slavery. "He sent Moses his servant and Aaron the man he had chosen" (105:26). Through them he worked miracles in Egypt until Pharaoh was glad to be rid of those troublemakers. Yahweh "led out Israel with silver and gold; in his tribes were none who fell behind" (105:37). The Israelites knew they were free when they saw the water of the sea covering their oppressors until not one of them was left alive. "Then they believed in God's words; then they sang his praises" (106:12).

Commenting on how the liberation from Egypt was transposed by biblical authors after the exile in Babylon, Louis Bouyer has said:

> Israel is tending toward freedom from that prison of stone which is the old heart of mankind born of Adam, for which a new heart is to be substituted, the heart of flesh in which Yahweh Himself will inscribe His law.[3]

Horizons of Liberation

The exodus and similar events in which we can trace the paradigm of liberation put us in touch with a very simple but exceedingly rich truth. The truth, about a people held in bondage finding freedom through God's liberating love, can be transposed on many different levels, for it transcends its expression in any particular historical circumstance. The underlying unity and simplicity of the biblical tradition appear when these basic lessons are understood with deepening insight down through the centuries. From the beginning, God has been a liberating, saving God, but the implications of this mystery have been seen and appreciated only gradually, as the people of God cried out for release from the manifold forms of their bondage. "He paid heed to their distress, so often as he heard their cry" (106:44).

In our own period of history, we know from the experiences of prisoners in World War II—such as Dietrich Bonhoeffer, Maximilian Kolbe, Alfred Delp, Edith Stein— that it is possible to be inwardly free even if one is held in physical bondage. There is a genre of deeply spiritual prison-journals that attest such freedom. Conversely, one can be outwardly free but interiorly living in bondage. The bonds that can enslave us are either obvious or subtle, and operative on many levels of our being. Once when Jesus was discussing freedom with a crowd at the temple treasury, he promised that living in the truth would set them free. They retorted that as descendants of Abraham they felt perfectly free and did not consider themselves enslaved in any way. Jesus answered them: "I give you my assurance, everyone who lives in sin is the slave of sin" (Jn 8:34).

Slavery to sin can be intertwined with numerous other forms of bondage. On the level of the physical senses, bondage may take the form of addiction to food, drugs, alcohol, sex, and even to aesthetic and artistic pleasures. On the social-cultural level we can be enslaved by greed for money, possessions, power, honor, security—all the things and people that we cling to and are afraid to lose. What we grasp and cannot let go of, holds us bound.[4] On the intellectual level, there are, for example, the certitudes we hold and that hold us within their clearly defined limits—at least until scientific evidence compels some revision. On the deepest level of the self, there are psychological and spiritual influences that operate on us from within, preconsciously, and condition our free decisions without taking away our human freedom totally. In the depths of the self we stand free to choose life or death. The paradox of freedom is that we are not fully free until we let go of our self, our life, at the center. Jesus put it this way: "Whoever would preserve his life will lose it, but whoever loses his life for my sake and the gospel's will preserve it" (Mk 8:35).

Jesus himself lived this paradox. The exaltation to glory that followed the crushing affliction of his passion was a sign that life, not death, has the final word. In the mystery of Christ we recognize both the afflicted one who is liberated from the bonds of death and at the same time the divine savior who accomplishes the effective liberation of humanity from sin. The songs of freedom in the psalter, by repeating the pattern of bondage and liberation in so many situations, seem to long for a final, decisive act of liberation by a saving God. Some of the psalms are explicit in their messianic expectation, celebrating in advance the victory of the Lord who will come to rule the earth:

> Let the land and all it bears rejoice,
>   all the trees of the wood shout for joy
> at the presence of the Lord for he comes,
>   he comes to rule the earth.
> With justice he will rule the world,
>   he will judge the people with his truth. (96:12-13)

Subsequent generations recognized the risen Christ as the Lord who calls all peoples of the world to freedom interiorly and exteriorly by proclaiming the truth that sets us free.

Concluding Example

In this chapter, the structure of the psalter's songs of freedom has emerged as a fourfold event. Out of affliction a cry for help is raised. The subsequent experience of being set free evokes an expression of gratitude and praise. These four elements constitute the paradigm of liberation, even though they need not all be present explicitly and in a predictable order. Variability and flexibility are signs of life and indications that the psalmists were expressing actual life experiences, not imitating literary paradigms. The fourfold recurring pattern that can be discerned in many of these experiences helps us better appreciate the structure of the event of liberation without turning the paradigm into a rigid mold for all experiences.

We wish to see the fourfold paradigm as a description that goes beyond the psalter and helps us understand not only other events in the Bible but also events that happen throughout history and even in our own lives. The major lessons of biblical revelation have a universal application. Wherever and whenever there are people living constricted lives, people crying out for freedom from oppression and exploitation, there we can expect a response of some sort from God our liberator and savior. When people experience that response as at least a partial release from bondage, then they have reason to celebrate. They know they are sustained by a mysterious power of liberating love.

As a concluding example of the flexibility of this paradigm in situations outside the psalter, there is a passage in the *Acts of the Apostles* that deserves attention. On his second missionary journey, Paul was thrown in prison at Philippi, along with his companion Silas, for disturbing the peace by his preaching. The jailer was told to guard them carefully, and he went so far as to chain their feet to a stake. In this situation of confinement and unjust affliction, Paul and Silas turned to God in prayer, prolonging their supplications far into the night, while the other prisoners who had endured maximum security much longer than these newcomers, watched, waited, and hoped. We are not told in what words Paul and Silas prayed, but the psalms that they knew by heart would have been appropriate. "Bring my soul out of this prison and then I shall praise your name. Around me the just will assemble because of your goodness to me" (142:8). At midnight, the God of liberation and compassion intervened with power:

About midnight, while Paul and Silas were praying and singing hymns to God as their fellow prisoners listened, a severe earthquake suddenly shook the place, rocking the prison to its foundations. Immediately all the doors flew open and everyone's chains were pulled loose. (Acts 16:25-26)

Immediate liberation! But before they could leave, the jailer appeared in the open doorway. Unable to see anything in the darkness, he imagined that his prisoners had escaped and was about to take his own life rather than face judiciary reprimand. "But Paul shouted to him, 'Do not harm yourself! We are all still here.' The jailer called for a light, then rushed in and fell trembling at the feet of Paul and

Silas" (Acts 16:28-29). Thus far, the story has moved rapidly from the experience of affliction in prison, to the prayer for rescue, to the liberating act of God that freed the prisoners from their chains. Next, the jailer himself was liberated from the bonds of paganism as he went through a sudden conversion to belief in the God whom Paul and Silas worshipped, whose power was so apparent. He and his whole household were baptized that very night. After this, we find the final step of the paradigm when heartfelt thanks were given to God in a context of eating and drinking: "The jailer led them up into his house, spread a table before them, and joyfully celebrated with his whole family his newfound faith in God" (Acts 16:34).

"God leads the prisoners forth into freedom" (Ps 68:7). Many of the psalms can be appreciated as songs of freedom. We now understand the basic structure of the experience of being set free, and have seen how the pattern recurs in a variety of situations. The progressive deepening of this insight will unfold its abundant implications.

NOTES

1. Albert Gelin, *The Psalms Are Our Prayers,* trans. Michael Bell (Collegeville, Minnesota: Liturgical Press, 1964), p. 23.
2. "In the ancient Near East this task represented the most tedious, strenuous, and common form of labor. Mud was hauled in baskets; finished bricks were carried in baskets. Basket-carrying as such was not characteristic of a definitive phase of labor. It was part of the building process from start to finish. It was a sign of servitude." Othmar Keel, *The Symbolism of the Biblical World,* trans. Timothy Hallett (New York: Seabury, Crossroad, 1978), pp. 271-272.
3. Louis Bouyer, *The Meaning of Sacred Scripture,* trans. Mary Perkins Ryan (Notre Dame, Indiana: University of Notre Dame Press, 1958), p. 231.
4. For the honest recognition of how an author can be enslaved to writing, see Etty Hillesum, *An Interrupted Life* (New York: Pantheon, 1983), p. 12.

CHAPTER FOUR

PRAYER IN IMAGES

The psalter is a school of prayer that teaches by example more than by academic explanations. We have seen that the second step in the typical pattern of a liberation experience is the cry for help, a prayer of petition; the final step is an expression of gratitude, a prayer of praise or thanksgiving. In this chapter we comb the psalter for its teaching on prayer, including forms of prayer that could be called contemplative. French theologian Louis Bouyer has said that the psalms are "the prayer by which the Spirit has taught us to ask exactly what the Father wishes to give us by His Son."[1]

The experience of unfreedom leads eventually to genuine prayer, if one is not resigned to endure the enslavement. Jesus in a most illuminating remark about freedom said, "If the son frees you, you will really be free" (Jn 8:36). In the act of prayer we ask to be set free by the Son. If we seek liberation from any source other than the Son of God, it will not be complete and lasting freedom.

Why is it that only the Son can set us free? To be set free from affliction is to find life, fulfillment, security. If we could give ourselves this freedom, the affliction would be no more than a passing inconvenience, like a headache that we could be rid of by taking an aspirin. But the experience of human affliction and enslavement in their myriad forms and degrees cannot be definitively taken away by an aspirin, or by any person or thing in this world.

Definitive liberation cannot come from human beings, money, perfect health, the discoveries of science, the joys of art, the pleasures of sensuality. All these are limited liberators because their promise of life, fulfillment, and security is limited. Limited liberators are not to be despised, but "only if the son frees you, will you really be free." Something in us that chafes at any form of bondage will always seek the experience of ultimate liberation that can come only from what is beyond the self, and beyond this world. Ultimate liberation can be given only by the transcendent Son of God. The seeking, desiring, crying out towards the beyond is prayer. "The Lord listens to the needy and does not spurn his servants in their chains" (69:34).

The Psalmists At Prayer

The psalms teach prayer by placing on our lips words that are the uninhibited outpouring of hearts totally open to God. The vocabulary and images evoked by these prayers are often concrete, vivid realities that could be observed in a a society that was predominantly rural and agricultural. Yet these images convey profound truths about the relationship between God and humanity. For example, the common sight of shepherds guiding their flocks to fresh grass and refreshing streams may have inspired the author of Psalm 23: "The Lord is my shepherd; there is nothing I shall want." The prayer is an unforgettable expression of trust in God's care and a commitment to walk the path of righteousness, but the language is without abstract terms.

To say that the psalmists preferred material images is not to say that they had no concept of spiritual realities. Material blessings were signs and symbols of the covenant relationship between God and his people in faith, hope and love. The psalmist could indeed ask for material goods, for a long and peaceful life with many descendants. But the psalmist could also long to see the face of God and offer his or her entire being in total surrender to the divine plan with praise and joy. To learn from the psalmists, we need to take their culturally conditioned mentality into account, and call upon our own creative imaginations to meet them at the many levels on which they moved.

As we begin to explore the psalter's teaching on prayer, we recall the public, liturgical nature of the majority of psalms. These prayers accompanied the sacred rituals, processions, sacrifices, blessings and festivals in Solomon's temple before the exile and in the second temple built by Zerubabel around 515 B.C. They were chanted by a soloist or by a choir, with musicians providing appropriate harmony on their instruments. Although some of these prayers are intensely personal, they were not collected and preserved primarily for private devotional use but for public worship, first in the temple and later also in the synagogue. The psalms belong to the people of God as a whole, and their spirituality is the patrimony of the entire people, not of an elite class. The original author was an individual, and the prayer reflects his or her own experience and relationship with God, but these psalms have since been ratified and appropriated by all the people of God as their own.

The psalter teaches the ways of prayer concretely and without systematic approaches or specialized vocabulary. We can find the reality but not the terminology of mysticism, prayer of quiet, prayer of union, acquired and infused contemplation. Such terms result from theological reflection on experiences described in the Bible and elsewhere. Contemplation is a general term for the loving union with God that all are invited to share. This intimate communion with God is already promised and included when the psalms speak of freedom, salvation, redemption, covenant, kingdom. The experience of contemplative prayer is offered and accepted when God declares, "You shall be my people, and I will be your God" (Ezek 36:28), and the psalmist responds, "We are his people, the sheep of his flock" (100:3).

When the psalmists pray, we do not find references to mystical phenomena such as ecstasy or the suspension of sensory awareness. These and other special effects of prayer depend on numerous factors of nature and grace, including the expectation of having such experiences and the example of others who may be having them. The essential contemplative experience of life shared with God takes place in the depths of one's being, in the heart, where we are not directly, consciously aware of what is happening; God in himself transcends the capacity of human perception in this life.

The life of prayer, life with God, is to some extent hidden from our own immediate observation, but it is a quality of life, a share in God's life given to all who have surrendered the depths of their hearts to him totally. God acts within, even though we cannot monitor everything that is going on in this experience of prayer. Praying is somewhat similar to the process of nutrition that goes on within us, nourishing us, making us live, even though we are not consciously aware of exactly what goes on in digestion, circulation, metabolism, and so on. We eat, and the rest follows according to program. In prayer, we learn to open our hearts so that God may fill us with all good things, even with himself: "Open wide your mouth and I will fill it" (81:11). The results will be evident in the course of time.

Praying With the Body

The psalmists prayed not only from their heart or head but with their whole self. Metaphors for prayer are boldly drawn from bodily experiences. Sometimes joy sweeps over the entire person at the presence of God: "My body and my heart faint for joy; God is my possession forever" (73:26). Sometimes prayer is an aching for God who is not yet fully possessed: "For you I long, for you my soul is thirsting; my body pines for you like a dry, weary land without water; (63:2). The image of thirst is evoked eloquently in Psalm 42: "Like the deer that yearns for running streams, so my soul is yearning for you, my God. My soul is thirsting for God, the God of my life" (42:2-3).

Sighing and groaning are expressions of prayer. "My years are spent with sighs," says the psalmist (31:11). Prisoners groan for their freedom: "Let the groans of the prisoners come before you" (79:11). The sharper the affliction, the louder the psalmist groaned for help:

> I cry aloud to God,
>   cry aloud to God that he may hear me.
> In the day of my distress I sought the Lord.
>   My hands were raised at night without ceasing;
>   my soul refused to be consoled.
> I remembered my God and I groaned. (77:2-4)

Fervent prayer rises through tears: "I am exhausted with my groaning; every night I drench my pillow with tears; I bedew my bed with weeping (6:7). God is close to the prayers of the heartbroken (34:19), and does not let a single tear go unnoticed: "You have kept a record of my tears (are they not written in your book?)" (56:9).

Through tears and darkness, the psalmist strained for a glimpse of coming relief: "My eyes yearn for your saving help" (119:123. "My eyes are wasted away from looking for my God" (60:4). God's coming at last is like a flash of lightning in the night: "In you is the source of life and in your light we see light" (36:10). One commentator has found in this verse a description of perfect union with the living God.[2]

The communion with God that the psalmist prayed for, and which the prayer already expresses, is a secure resting in the divine embrace. Several psalms allude to the sheltering arms of God under the figure of wings as on the winged figures in the sanctuary of the temple: "In the shadow of your wings I rejoice" (63:7). Or the figure may be the arms of a mother holding her child in calm contentment: "Truly I have set my soul in silence and peace. A weaned child on its mother's breast even so is my soul" (131:2). Or a lover's embrace: "My soul clings to you; your right hand holds me fast" (63:9). In this verse the "right hand" recalls an image from the *Song of Songs* (Ct 8:3), while the verb for "cling" is used in Genesis 2:24 to describe how a man "clings to his wife, and the two of them become one body." The psalmist clings to God in a faithful union of covenant love: "I bind myself to do your will, Lord: do not disappoint me" (119:31). And God replies: "Since he clings to me in love, I will free him" (91:14).

Another sensual image for prayer is eating and drinking in the Lord's presence as a symbol of shared life. Some of the psalms refer to feasting on the occasion of the monthly full moon (81:3-4), or after the offering of a sacrifice in the temple: "They feast on the riches of your house; they drink from the stream of your delight" (36:9). To this festive meal

God invites the poor, for "the poor shall eat and shall have their fill" (22:27). "He satisfies the thirsty soul; he fills the hungry with good things" (107:9). When God acts as the host at the banquet, he opens his generous hand (104:28), gives bread to the needy (132:15), anoints their head with perfumed oil, and fills their cup to overflowing (23:5). There is no limit to the good things God is prepared to pour into a receptive heart. "Israel I would feed with finest wheat and fill them with honey from the rock" (81:16). The only limit is in our receptivity and openness, our readiness of heart. The psalmist's heart was a hungry void that no created person or possession could fill, but only the promise of God's coming. "Your promise is sweeter to my taste than honey in the mouth" (119:103). The psalmist held that posture of instant receptivity to God's loving gift of himself, and that posture was prayer of the heart. "My heart is ready, O God, my heart is ready" (57:8).

An Undivided Heart

The psalmists prayed with their bodies, but their prayer sprang from the heart: "My heart is ready, O God; I will sing, sing your praise" (108:2). The heart turned toward God will normally direct the body in the suitable manner of praying. What we find in the psalms is a heart centered inseparably on God, an undivided heart. Since it is God who enables us to pray at all, the psalmist asked for an appropriate transformation of heart, "A pure heart create for me, O God" (51:12), using the verb "create" with its resonances from the creation-narratives of Genesis.

The psalmists struck a high note of religious feeling by insisting that their heart's happiness lay in God alone. "In

God alone be at rest, my soul" (62:6). "What else have I in
heaven but you? Apart from you I want nothing on earth.
My body and my heart faint for joy; God is my possession
for ever. ... To be near God is my happiness" (73:25-28).
"I say to the Lord: 'You are my God. My happiness lies in
you alone' " (16:2). The psalmist counted on God's love
even more than on the love of father and mother, and asked
"to live in the house of the Lord all the days of my life, to
savor the sweetness of the Lord, to behold his temple"
(27:4, 10).

The intimacy of the psalmist's relationship with God in
prayer was like strolling with a close friend down a path
leading to the fullness of life. "I was always in your
presence; you were holding me by my right hand. You will
guide me by your counsel and so you will lead me to glory"
(73:23-24). The psalmist wished to be like the patriarch
Enoch who "walked with God and was no longer here, for
God took him" (Gen 5:24). The journey that begins in
prayer ends in everlasting happiness: "You will show me the
path of life, the fullness of joy in your presence, at your
right hand happiness forever" (16:11).

The favor of enjoying God's presence belongs to the pure
of heart. Such purity is the result of direct purification by
God through testing, as the fidelity of the Israelites was
tested in the desert for forty years, but it is also the result of
honest effort to deal justly and truthfully, doing no wrong
to a neighbor (15: 2-5). Prayer that is directed from a pure
heart wins quick assurance of God's presence: "When he
calls I shall answer, 'I am with you' " (91:15).

The pure, undivided heart seeks to gaze upon the face of
God. "The Lord is just and loves justice; the upright shall
see his face" (11:7). In the psalter, God's face signifies the
divine favor or blessing, as if God were smiling on his ser-

vant. The priestly blessing given by Aaron included this petition: "The Lord let his face shine upon you, and be gracious
to you!" (Num 6:25). God's blessing meant life in all its
forms and abundance, and it was this blessing that the
psalmists desired by constantly seeking God's face (105:4).
"Let your face shine on your servant; save me in your love"
(31:17). "O God be gracious and bless us and let your face
shed its light upon us" (67:2). In Psalm 80, the refrain is
repeated three times: "Let your face shine on us and we
shall be saved" (80:4, 8, 20).

When the bliss of God's nearness was not experienced, it
seemed to the psalmist that God had turned away his face.
"You hide your face, they are dismayed" (104:29). The
psalmist then prayed with redoubled fervor: "Of you my
 heart has spoken: 'Seek his face.' It is your face, O Lord,
that I seek; hide not your face" (27:8). God is not at the
beck and call of creatures, and the vision of his face is given
and withdrawn to show that it is sheer gift. In prayer, even
when there is a sense that God's face is turned toward us
lovingly and protectively, we still cannot make out the
features of that face; God remains dark mystery. To seek
the face of God is to know the alternation between God's
nearness and distance but always against the dark
background of impenetrable mystery.

Nearness and Distance

The experience of prayer over a long period of time alternates between consolation and desolation. The events of
daily life affect this alternation, because prayer is not
separate from concrete events but part of the context of daily life. The psalmists trusted that God would never abandon

them. In the midst of worries and cares, they were confident that they could count on God's presence and nearness: "When cares increase in my heart, your consolation calms my soul" (94:19).

The author of Psalm 30 felt that he or she understood the principle of alternation well enough: "God's anger lasts a moment; his favor all through life. At night there are tears, but joy comes with dawn" (30:6). Favor and joyfulness seemed to triumph most of the time, and the psalmist looked toward the future with serenity: "I said to myself in my good fortune: 'Nothing will ever disturb me' " (30:7). Suddenly the curtain came down on that happy scene. The precise nature of the calamity is not indicated, but could have been physical illness, unexpected loss, opposition from enemies, to the extent that death seemed likely. Where was God now? Where was the favor of his countenance? "Your favor had set me on a mountain fastness, then you hid your face and I was put to confusion" (30:8). God had apparently withdrawn his blessings so that the psalmist might learn how to distinguish better between blessings and the one who blesses, between consolations and the consoler, so as to love and serve God for himself alone. The desolate psalmist cried out to God in protest, made appeals to God's kindness, argued and bargained and finally surrendered to God's will. At that moment of truth, God made his presence felt once more. "The Lord listened and had pity; the Lord came to my help" (30:11). The psalm concludes on a note of gladness and thanksgiving because of the timely liberation. The psalmist's relationship with God resumed on a more mature level, with deeper faith, love and purity of heart. "For me you have changed my mourning into dancing. You removed my sackcloth and girded me with joy" (30:12).

The pattern of alternating desolation and consolation—from mourning in sackcloth to dancing with joy—is frequent in the psalter because it is a common experience in the life of prayer. When all goes smoothly, God's nearness seems obvious and immutable; then a major difficulty occurs, God seems to have abandoned his servant, and all the lights go out obliging one to pray in the dark if at all. God is playing an infuriating game of hide and seek. "Lord, why do you stand afar off and hide yourself in times of distress?" asked the psalmist (10:1). "Lord, why do you reject me? Why do you hide your face?" (88:15). "Awake, O Lord, why do you sleep? Arise, do not reject us forever! Why do you hide your face and forget our oppression and misery?" (44:24-25). In spite of these impassioned pleas, the only answer may be silence. The pleading goes on to no effect: Lord, answer; do not be silent; answer quickly for I am in distress; come close; "do not hide from my pleading, attend to me and reply; with my cares, I cannot rest" (55:2-3).

When every tactic fails to move God, the psalmist realizes that Yahweh is not like the pagan gods who can be cajoled and manipulated. Nor is God likely to appear and act so unmistakably that no other interpretation may be given, and faith may be replaced by certitude. In this experience of desolation, the one who chooses to go on praying is driven back to the limit of his or her faith, to the point of utter powerlessness where one can only accept and trust what one does not understand. God's ways are not our ways, but God's ways are always lovingly ordered to the greatest benefit of his servants and the greatest glory of his own name. "Our God is in the heavens; he does whatever he wills" (115:3). The psalmist's deepest prayer is saying "Yes" to God's will, whatever that might mean in the present circumstances.

Until the will of God changes sackcloth to garments of dancing, the psalmist's most cherished certitude was the faithful presence of God among the people to whom he had bound himself by an unbreakable covenant of love. "Even though the waters rage and foam, even though the mountains be shaken by its waves, the Lord of hosts is with us; the God of Jacob is our stronghold," says the refrain of Psalm 46 (46:4, 8, 12). The author of Psalm 37 advised people to take the long view, remaining patient and calm, trusting instead of fretting over the present misfortune. God will act eventually, the author promised, and on that day of liberation "your justice will break forth like the light, your cause like the noon-day sun" (37:6). For now, the best advice is: "Be still before the Lord and wait in patience" (37:6).

Watching and Waiting

"The Lord delights in those who revere him, in those who wait for his love" (147:11). The reality of the life of prayer is that the moments of exaltation when we dance to a new song are high peaks on a vast plain of ordinariness. It is no different from everyday life where the periodic holidays stand out as celebrations because the ordinary context is commonplace working and living. Growth in the life of prayer takes place by barely noticeable differences, to the frustration of those who expect instant effects. Techniques and methods of praying are useful to dispose the heart and mind for the encounter with God, but cannot of themselves produce that encounter. The relationship of prayer is not under the control and management of the human partner.

The psalmists discovered that their role in the relationship with God was often more receptive and passive than active.

The principle is an important one because it does not imply being unfeeling or coldly indifferent but means accepting God as total liberator. The psalmists did not liberate themselves but were liberated by God's strong hand and outstretched arm. Their part was to hold themselves in readiness, watching, waiting, trusting God's power and willingness to act on their behalf. "How great is the goodness, Lord, that you keep for those who fear you, that you show to those who trust you in the sight of men. You hide them in the shelter of your presence, . . . you keep them safe within your tent" (31:20-21).

Patient waiting for the Lord is not an impassive stance but an attitude of quiet receptivity. The psalmist searched for God gently and trustingly, not with an anxious, driven, desperate spirit. There can be strong passion that does not express itself by hysterics but by steady watchfulness like a watchman waiting for dawn: "My soul is waiting for the Lord, I count on his word. My soul is longing for the Lord more than watchman for daybreak" (130:5-6). "In the morning I offer you my prayer, watching and waiting" (5:4).

The time for waiting for the Lord in prayer is often filled with mental or vocal words, but silence is its most perfect expression. "Truly I have set my soul in silence and peace," says the psalmist (131:2). There is a tendency to believe that acceptable prayer must be phrased in exactly the right way in order to catch God's attention and appeal to him irresistibly. We make speeches that seem stunning in eloquence, to ourselves. There is no need for speeches or for elaborate mental reflections when the heart is firmly centered on God in love and trust. The fourteenth-century English spiritual master, Richard Rolle, said: "We pray truly then when we do not think about anything, but our whole will is directed toward the highest things, and our soul is set ablaze with the fire of the Holy Spirit."[3] The psalter puts it in a single line by having Yahweh say: "Be still and know that I am God" (45:11). In the context of this psalm, the injunction "Be still" carries the meaning of: be at rest, be silent, leave off struggling and fighting, do nothing more for yourself. In that experience of doing nothing, God will manifest himself and do everything: "You will know that I am God."

Waiting in silence gives the psalmist time to listen. "Listen, my people, I will speak," says the Lord (50:7). The word by which God reveals himself is as delicate as the sound of the gentle breeze that Elijah heard on Mount Horeb (1 Kgs 19:12). It can be heard when there is silence exteriorly and in the emotions and desires and chattering of the imagination. The psalmist practiced this discipline: "I was silent, not opening my lips" (39:10). Jesus himself practiced this silence when he refused to defend himself before his accusers at his trial. A servant of God who waits in silence and trust, does not wait for his or her own benefit alone, but waits for God to bring about a kingdom of freedom and love for all people. In the silence of total surrender to God's will, a new creation is being shaped for the one who prays and for the whole world. The self-emptying of silence opens on a life of radical freedom.

Conclusion

Prayer from the heart can result in the experience of being re-created for a life of freedom. How free is a person really willing to be? We are prepared to pray, especially in situations of affliction and bondage, but are we prepared to accept responsibility for the result of our answered prayers? Some degree of bondage almost seems preferable to the strangeness and risk of living in freedom as servants of God alone. American psychiatrist Fritz Kunkel has said, "We live in a jail we call our castle." We think we are better off in our so-called castle, and resist emerging fully into the spaciousness of life in freedom.

God the liberator, who is the one we face in the relationship of prayer, not only frees those who ask but even calls us to a life of freedom. "He leads the prisoners forth into freedom" (68:7). "He brought me forth into freedom" (18:20). Psalm 22 reflects on God's role in the psalmist's birth: "It was you who took me from the womb" (22:10). The event of birth is everyone's first experience of passing through the narrow way that leads from the dark enclosure of the womb out into the freedom of independent existence. The psalmist pictured the liberating God as a midwife drawing the child from the womb. Prayer is a rebirth experience in which God draws us forth into freedom again and again. Prayer is letting oneself be drawn from a comfortable and secure burrow in order to reach new stages of growth in the open space of freedom amid new relationships. In time, that new stage of maturity becomes too cramped and narrow, and God calls us forth once more to rebirth in freedom. At every stage, there is a chance that we will prefer the familiar prison and refuse to be set free.

As we conclude these reflections on the psalmists' way of praying, we need to ask if we are willing to take the psalmists as our models. Would we rather remain in the land of unfreedom—in our Egypt where we have learned to cope with fears, inhibitions, taboos, and restrictive shackles—or will we follow the Lord across the desert into the land of freedom? The freedom of the promised land is not a license to live as we please but the freedom to accept God's will trustingly and unconditionally. It is the freedom to live by God's spirit of love as the source of meaning and responsibility in the concrete situation. Such freedom may cost us our sense of security coming from predictable patterns of living, but it empowers us to turn to God for help in all circumstances, to be genuine with God in love and sometimes in anger, to rely on God's unseen presence for support and ultimate security. Freedom includes permission to accept ourselves as made in God's image, accept our feelings, accept our failings. Freedom also includes an invitation to dream and to make choices and lifetime commitments that will help that dream come true. In all these ways we move from exterior freedom to that inner freedom of heart which is the love that casts out all fear. The psalms are always at hand as songs of freedom and models of prayer.

NOTES

1. Louis Bouyer, *The Meaning of Sacred Scripture,* trans. Mary Perkins Ryan (Notre Dame, Indiana: University of Notre Dame Press, 1958), p. 227.

2. H. J. Franken, *The Mystical Communion With JHWH in the Book of Psalms* (Leiden: E. J. Brill, 1954), p. 25: "Psalm 36:10 reaches the highest possible degree of unity with God, when speaking of the light, as the most intimate relation." Psalm 36:10 may be compared to the description of the heavenly Jerusalem in the final book of the New Testament: "The city had no need of sun or moon, for the glory of God gave it light, and its lamp was the Lamb" (Rev 21:23). Compare also this image from the Hindu Upanishads speaking of the world beyond: "The sun does not shine there, nor the moon nor the stars nor these lightnings, much less this earthly fire. When He shines, everything shines after Him, by His light all this is enlightened" (quoted by Bede Griffiths, *The Cosmic Revelation* [Springfield, Illinois: Templegate, 1983], p. 84).

3. Richard Rolle, *The Fire of Love,* trans. M. L. de Mastro (Garden City, New York: Image Books, 1981), p. 69.

CHAPTER FIVE

PROFILES OF THE FREE

"Tell me what you read, and I'll tell you who you are." There are several variations of this proverbial wisdom: Tell me your friends, or your dreams, or your favorite foods, and I will tell you who you are. We reveal ourselves still more completely in our prayers. The psalms are prayers born in the hearts of the free, or those longing for freedom, and they reveal much about the men and women who originally prayed this way. Because the psalms also express universal human attitudes of prayer, they sketch a profile that is not limited to the original authors.

A gap of many generations and many cultural differences separates us from the Hebrew psalmists in the centuries before Christ, yet we can see in the psalms, as in a mirror, the attitudes we ourselves may or should have when we turn to God in prayer. French exegete Albert Gelin identified some of these attitudes when he wrote:

> The faithful Jew prayed for salvation, that is to say, at that period, a long and happy life, the goods of this earth, protection against enemies, deliverance from distress; he prayed for *shalom,* peace, that is, a flowering-out in the good things of this world; he prayed for *baraka,* blessing, which is more or less equivalent to vitality, fruitfulness. He prayed with hope.[1]

What the psalmists prayed for and the way they prayed can be described in some detail. The present chapter explores both the positive and negative features of the profile that results. The features are gathered from many different psalms and do not necessarily apply in the same degree to all the psalmists and to all who pray. Nevertheless, the positive aspects will be recognized as fairly typical characteristics of deeply prayerful, liberated persons whom we know from historical biographies or personal encounters.

Just

The first psalm of the psalter contrasts the way of the just with the way of the wicked. The wicked are destined for doom: "They like winnowed chaff shall be driven away by the wind" (1:4). Anyone who is just in God's sight "is like a tree that is planted beside the flowing waters, that yields its fruit in due season and whose leaves shall never fade" (1:3). With this image in the opening psalm like an overture, the psalter introduces its principal character, the just one, the one who is pleasing to Yahweh.

To call someone just or righteous today would not do justice to the psalter's presentation of the just one. Today a just person is someone who treats others fairly, without favoritism or discrimination, dealing squarely with all according to principles. In the psalter, the just one is the person who is pleasing to God in everything. Psalm 1 pronounced a blessing on the just one "whose delight is the law of the Lord and who ponders his law day and night" (1:2).[2]

The just one does not stop at pondering and delighting over God's law as if it were a priceless treasure to be admired. The just one lives by God's law, scrutinizing it only in order to understand, assimilate, and obey it in its entirety. The just are pleasing to God because they are faithful to all the demands of his law. "It is the Lord who loves the just but thwarts the path of the wicked" (146:8-9).

The piety of the just can seem to be evidence of a rigidly legalistic mentality unless we understand that God's law means more than the ten commandments and the prescriptions governing liturgical cult. God's law includes explicit precepts such as these but goes beyond them in two ways. First, external practices are expected to reflect interior dispositions. The living God has no need of ritual offerings of food. "Were I hungry I would not tell you, for I own the world and all it holds. Do you think I eat the flesh of bulls, or drink the blood of goats?" (50:12-13). God loathes gestures or prayers that do not flow from purity of heart and compassion. "For in sacrifice you take no delight, burnt offering from me you would refuse; my sacrifice, a contrite spirit. A humbled, contrite heart you will not spurn" (51:18-19).

God's law goes beyond explicit precepts in a second way, because law (or instruction, *torah*) is another name for the all-encompassing divine will. The just one surrenders to God's will, trusts God's will, finds true peace and happiness in God's will. Such is the great theme which opens the psalter and comes back implicitly or explicitly as a refrain in all 150 psalms. "In the scroll of the book it stands written that I should do your will. My God, I delight in your law in the depth of my heart" (40:8-9). The psalmists found many synonyms for the will of God, such as law, word, statute, decree, command, but beneath them all is the delight that pulsates in the depths of the heart of the just.

Psalm 119 has a reference to God's will, under one name or another, in all but two of its 176 verses. "I rejoiced to do your will as though all riches were mine" (119:14). This treasure is called "song in the land of exile," truth that "lasts from age to age," sweeter to the taste "than honey in the mouth," a lamp and a light for the path (119:54, 90, 103, 105). The poetic structure of this lengthy psalm follows an intricate pattern in which each letter of the Hebrew alphabet is used as the beginning letter of eight consecutive verses. C. S. Lewis described it as "a thing done like embroidery, stitch by stitch, through long, quiet hours, for love of the subject and for the delight in leisurely, disciplined craftsmanship."[3]

God's will as Torah is celebrated against a cosmic background in Psalm 19. Although some prefer to see two distinct psalms juxtaposed here, the first glorifying God in sun, earth, and sky, and the second praising God's law, the psalmist's poetic vision could easily have embraced both aspects. The same divine will guides the course of the heavens and of human events, and there is nothing concealed from the burning sun or from the provisions of God's law. God's law, which is always an exhortation to "turn away from evil and do good" (37:27), is a sign of God's loving care for his people. The law is to be loved and trusted as a source of life and freedom: "I will never forget your precepts for with them you give me life" (119:93). "You will show me the path of life" (16:11). The law is like the shepherd's crook and staff, gently guiding the just one along the right path, comforting, protecting, refreshing, providing (Psalm 23).

The just one, compared in Psalm 1 to a fruitful tree beside the flowing waters, is rooted in the divine will. Temples in the ancient Near East were often landscaped with trees, pools, and flowing streams. The just one of Psalm 52 says: "I am like a growing olive tree in the house of God" (52:10). To the author of Psalm 92, the just resemble the stately palm-tree or the towering cedar: "The just will flourish like the palm-tree and grow like a Lebanon cedar.

Planted in the house of the Lord they will flourish in the courts of our God, still bearing fruit when they are old, still full of sap, still green'' (92:13-15).

The fruitfulness of the life of the just one depends on uninterrupted contact with the flowing stream of God's will that directs the course of events on earth as it does in heaven. Circumstances and people interact in predictable or completely unpredictable ways, but the providential divine plan surrounds all human history and orders it to the glory of God. Those whom the psalter calls just are people who have surrendered themselves completely to God's mysterious plan of love for them. Such surrender does not come easily, because there is nothing more difficult than to let go of one's own free choice or will in favor of someone else's will, someone else's law. The just have made that offering, without bargaining or setting conditions, and have found favor with God. "Teach me to do your will for you, O Lord, are my God" (143:10).

At first glance it may seem that the just one loses all personal freedom. After putting all one's power of free choice into a lifelong commitment to God's will, what is there left of liberty? This dilemma, which the mind sees and fears, is best resolved by the actual experience of surrendering. At first, God's will appears as constraint or limit. Gradually, the just one discovers that it was self-will that was lost, not freedom. The choice of saying "Yes" to God's will is a choice that opens out on the infinite vistas of the divine plan in the spaciousness of true freedom. God's will is not a narrow track but a broad highway down which the just one runs with carefree heart. "I will run the way of your commands; you give freedom to my heart" (119:32).

Poor

The poor who appear in the psalms share many of the qualities of the just, but with a different emphasis. In actual life, the just were often the poor, and the poor were often the just ones. Psalm 34 alternates the two terms almost interchangeably. The equivalence is not complete, however, for the just may lack the spirit of the poor. The virtue of the just is open to faults of complacency. Like the elder son in the parable of the father and two sons, the just one may take pride in his years of faithful service, saying, "I never disobeyed one of your orders" (Lk 15:29). The poor would not be inclined to take credit for their own fidelity, or take it for granted, or forget that they were doing no more than their duty (Lk 17:10).

In Hebrew, the plural form *anawim* is the usual term for the category of the poor in the psalter. The psalmists often included themselves in this category. According to the French Oratorian, Louis Bouyer:

> As has been said, following St. Augustine, the psalms are only, from one end to the other, the prayer of the "poor," those *anawim* to whom the Beatitudes promise the kingdom of heaven, who know that man has nothing that he can be proud of before God, but also nothing that he may not hope for from his mercy.[4]

At times the psalmists generalized, and equated the poor with all the people of Israel, or at least with the remnant fully open to God's liberating, saving power: "The Lord takes delight in his people; he crowns the poor with salvation" (149:4).

How poor were the poor of the psalms? Sometimes the poor are identified as widows, orphans, the hungry, the weak, the wretched. These people were economically powerless and dependent on others. Today they would include the whole class of the underprivileged, and especially the down-and-out destitute. References to the poor never quite abandon this economic or sociological meaning, but a more religious meaning became primary. The poor were those who relied on God rather than on their own resources. The author of Psalm 86 cried out: "Turn your ear, O Lord, and give answer for I am poor and needy. Preserve my life, for I am faithful: save the servant who trusts in you" (86:1-2). This shift from an economic to a predominantly religious meaning parallels a similar shift in meaning when the psalms talk about the rich. "The opposite of the *anawim* were not simply the rich, but the proud and self-sufficient who showed no need of God or His help."⁵ The poor are helpless before the mighty, whom the psalmists called wicked and sinners: "The poor man is devoured by the pride of the wicked" (10:1).

The distinction between economic poverty and religious or spiritual poverty is significant because the psalms in general do not extol indigence as a spiritual value. The psalmists loved life along with all its material blessings, and they were tempted to cast an envious eye at the rich (73:3). The recognized, however, that their true liberator was God, and that material wealth and power were unreliable. "They shall laugh and say: 'So this is the man who refused to take God as his stronghold, but trusted in the greatness of his wealth' " (52:8-9). At the same time, the psalmists knew that economic poverty sometimes leads to resentment or despair, and is not necessarily a privileged path to spiritual poverty. Spiritual poverty is compatible with ownership because it consists in a basic freedom of heart that trusts in God rather than in possessions. "Do not set your heart on riches even when they increase. For God has said only one thing: only two do I know: that to God alone belongs power and to you Lord, love; and that you repay each one according to his deeds" (62:11-12).

Psalm 37 promised bravely, "The *anawim* shall inherit the land!" (37:11). Since the *anawim* were not in a position to inherit much of anything, this promise was a bold act of trust in the power of Yahweh to reverse the fortunes of the poor or to give them a place in his own heavenly land. For the poor, whose eyes were always on the Lord God until he showed them his mercy (123:3), the primary landscape of their life was God. The New Testament lifted this verse verbatim from the psalter and placed it in the beatitudes as a description of those who will inherit the kingdom of God: "Blest are the lowly; they shall inherit the land" (Mt 5:4). The first beatitude—"How blest are the poor in spirit: the reign of God is theirs" (Mt 5:3)—emphasized the same basic paradox. Total dependence on God is the path to total freedom.

The poor are blest because God will do for them what they are unable to do for themselves. The psalmists never tired of repeating such promises. "From the dust he lifts up the lowly, from the dungheap he raises the poor" (113:7). "He shall save the poor when they cry and the needy who are helpless. He will have pity on the weak and save the lives of the poor" (72:12-13). "The Lord listens to the needy and does not spurn his servants in their chains" (69:34). "He stands at the poor man's side to save him from those who condemn him" (109:30). "I know the Lord will avenge the poor, that he will do justice for the needy" (140:13).

The French exegete Albert Gelin, after studying the theme of the *anawim* in both the Hebrew and Christian scriptures, believed that over the centuries the term acquired an aura of meaning that cannot be captured in a single word or phrase.[6] The poor are humble before God in their inability to liberate themselves. They seek the Lord and wait for his salvation. "My soul is waiting for the Lord" (130:5). The poor know how to wait, with openness and trust. The poor in our modern cities are like the *anawim* in this respect, for they have no other choice but to wait: for medical care, for jobs, for public transportation, for food stamps and social security checks, for free meals.

The *anawim* are sustained in their waiting by prayer and expectation. "Turn to me and have mercy," they beg, "for I am lonely and poor" (25:16). The prayer of the poor is not the prayer of whimpering beggers whose spirit has been crushed or embittered by hardship, but the prayer of those who have been seasoned by life's experiences and have become mature, gentle, compassionate people completely abandoned to God's will. They pray with the purity, simplicity, and interior littleness of a child: "O search me, God, and know my heart. O test me and know my thoughts. See that I follow not the wrong path and lead me in the path of life eternal" (139:23-24).

The poor are not people who have lost hope because the world has forgotten them, but people who have placed all their hope in God: "The needy shall not always be forgotten nor the hopes of the poor be in vain" (9:19). They are not joyless, gloomy people but joyful in their certitude of God's wisdom and eventual intervention: "The poor when they see it will be glad, and God-seeking hearts will revive" (69:33). "He has never despised nor scorned the poverty of the poor.

From him he has not hidden his face, but he heard the poor one when he cried" (22:25). The poverty of the *anawim* is freedom and joy. They not only acknowledge their dependence but recognize that the condition of unqualified clinging to God is their greatest security.

Afflicted

The radical poverty of the *anawim* implies a renunciation of one's resources which does not come naturally. People naturally fear such denudation. They accept it only when there is no other choice, only when they are obliged to say: "My life is spent with sorrow and my years with sighs. Affliction has broken down my strength" (31:11). Voluntary poverty is not often found in comfortable circumstances; more often it is the result of affliction in some form. Suffering teaches lessons that are scarcely learned in any other way. "It was good for me to be afflicted, to learn your statutes" (119:71). The psalmists walked before the Lord in freedom and simplicity of heart because their heart had been pierced within them by affliction: "The Lord is close to the broken-hearted" (34:19; 109:22).

Nearly every possible form of misfortune seems to have befallen the psalmists. The psalms of lament are sometimes an unending litany of woe. The psalmist was devastated with misery, exhausted from sighing, from tears that waste the eyes, a parched throat, and a tongue that cleaves to the jaws in fear. "I am a reproach, an object of scorn to my neighbors and of fear to my friends. Those who see me in the street run far away from me. I am like a thing thrown away" (31:12-13). There was absolutely no human consolation or defense, no means of escape, "not one who cares for

my soul" (142:5). A commentator has written, without exaggeration:

> There is surely no sentiment of a suffering soul that has
> not its place in the Psalms. Sometimes the supplication is
> calm and serene, sometimes it is accompanied with a note of
> impatience, sometimes it is expressed with pathetic
> vehemence, sometimes it is so agonised as to border on
> despair. The psalmists were men, poor men of flesh and
> blood grappling with all the trials that torture fallen
> humanity.[7]

It seems almost possible to conclude from some passages
that the psalmists were paranoid, suffering from an appall-
ing persecution-complex. Psychoanalysis across the centuries is risky. Who knows what objective factors were making life difficult for these psalmists? What we do know is
that we are dealing with poetic forms which use imagery to
convey meaning vividly and forcefully. The psalmists felt afflicted and oppressed to the point that their only refuge was
God. The cause of their affliction was usually projected outward and objectified in the form of nameless "foes,"
"evildoers," "the wicked."

The afflicted felt themselves the target of verbal abuse
and calumny from foes "whose mouths are filled with lies,
whose hands are raised in perjury" (144:8). "They sharpen
their tongues like swords; they aim bitter words like arrows
to shoot at the innocent from ambush, shooting suddenly
and recklessly" (64:4-5). The psalmist prayed to be
delivered from these schemers "who plan evil in their hearts
and stir up strife every day; who sharpen their tongue like an
adder's with the poison of viper on their lips" (140:3-4). In
some cases, malice moved from words to lethal actions, and
the psalmist knew he was no match for their strength: "My

foes encircle me with deadly intent. ... They advance against me, and now they surround me. Their eyes are watching to strike me to the ground as though they were lions ready to claw or like some young lion crouched in hiding" (17:9-12). The comparisons to savage beasts reverberate with ferocity: "Many bulls have surrounded me, fierce bulls of Bashan close me in. Against me they open wide their jaws, like lions, rending and roaring. ... Many dogs have surrounded me, a band of the wicked beset me. . . . Save my life from the jaws of these lions, my poor soul from the horns of these oxen" (22:13, 17, 22).

Another frequent image is the hunter's trap. "The proud have hidden a trap, have spread out lines in a net, set snares across my path" (140:6). "They have hidden a net for me wantonly; they have dug a pit" (35:7). The image of a trap was borrowed from the primitive method of hunting by means of a pitfall covered with camouflaged nets. Snares were also used for catching birds (124:7). These traps caused much psychological fear because they could not be detected, and to fall into them meant irreversible disaster. The psalmist's fondest wish was to see his adversaries fall suddenly into their own trap: "Let the wicked fall into the traps they have set whilst I pursue my way unharmed" (141:10; 35:8). The trap most to be feared was death itself, which no one escapes, but the afflicted hoped for a reprieve: "The waves of death rose about me; the torrents of destruction assailed me; the snares of the grave entangled me; the traps of death confronted me. In my anguish I called to the Lord: I cried to my God for help" (18:5-7).

The afflicted ones of the psalter and down through the ages found themselves trapped in desperate situations. The limits of the trap are the limits of human freedom in concrete circumstances. Psalm 107 describes four cases of apparently hopeless entrapment: wanderers lost in the desert, prisoners in misery and chains, the terminally ill, and sailors caught in a storm at sea. In each incident the afflicted "cried to the Lord in their need and he rescued them from their distress" (107: 6, 13, 19, 28). God set them free from the trap as soon as he was given an opening, an invitation to intervene and transform the situation. The afflicted who call upon God discover how their trap—their helplessness, confusion, and inability to make things right again—is the very condition of God's liberating, saving activity. The first step is to stop thrashing about desperately in the trap, which usually leads to further entanglement. The next step is to call for help from the only source that can make some sense out of the most constraining situations.

Some traps will have to be lived with or lived in because they are the results of past free choices or larger political and economic structures.[8] However, the attitude with which we face these constraints can be liberated by the transforming power and presence of God. The author of Psalm 107 invited the wise to heed these examples and "consider the love of the Lord" (107:43). The psalmist's adversaries mocked all appeals to a divine liberator: "How many are saying about me: 'There is no help for him in God' " (3:3). The afflicted one knew better: "As for me, I trust in the Lord: let me be glad and rejoice in your love. You who have seen my affliction and taken heed of my soul's distress, have not handed me over to the enemy, but set my feet at large" (31:8-9). Affliction may be the path to spiritual freedom.

The psalms, however, cannot be used to justify conditions of oppression and injustice that bring about a lifetime of affliction for the poor. The liberating God who led Israel out of slavery in Egypt does not expect his people to appreciate and adapt to injustice.[9] The most evident proof for this fact in the psalter can be found in what are called the cursing psalms. These psalms or portions of psalms hurl imprecations at the enemy with typical semitic passion and hyperbole. "O God, break the teeth in their mouths, tear out the fangs of these wild beasts, O Lord!" (58:7). "Let coals of fire rain upon them. Let them be flung in the abyss, no more to rise" (140:11). The afflicted did not take their troubles lightly. The first reaction of many was to strike back with a curse. The same person at other times or other people under the same circumstances might show more patience and self-control. There are also many examples of blessing in the psalter as will be seen in a later section. The afflicted who curse have good reason, and those who call upon the Lord have good reason also: judgment and mercy are both in the hands of the Lord. Those who remember the ultimate liberator find some measure of peace in affliction.

Inner Peace

Scattered throughout the psalms are bloodthirsty curses, calls to combat, the warcry and the battle trumpet, descriptions of violence and strife. God is invoked as the liberator with superior forces at his command. Even the world of nature is sometimes described as the scene of cosmic struggles between untamed monsters (74:14). When the psalmist's heart is laid bare, we may see that it is full of restless thoughts and turbulent emotions, like "the sea, vast and wide, with its moving swarms past counting, living things great and small'' (104:25).

At the same time, the psalmists yearned for peace, sang of peace, prayed for peace, wished peace to one another, and declared themselves unhesitatingly on the side of peace. "Long enough have I been dwelling with those who hate peace. I am for peace, but when I speak, they are for fighting" (120:6-7). They claimed to lose no sleep to restlessness and worry: "I will lie down in peace and sleep comes at once" (4:9). They knew that the deepest source of peace lies in embracing God's will as expressed in daily circumstances and in the precepts of the law: "The lovers of your law have great peace" (119:165).

It is not always easy to reconcile the apparently contradictory tendencies towards war and peace in the psalter, and to bring into focus the true profile of a devout, liberated servant of the Lord. The 1983 pastoral letter of the American Catholic bishops on "The Challenge of Peace: God's Promise and Our Response" attempted to reconcile the biblical texts by referring to an evolution that took place gradually over the centuries.[10] In the early stage of Israel's covenant with God, the metaphor of God as a liberating warrior expressed trust and security in an invincible protector who would defend their small nation as he had done in the past. In the course of time, especially after the exile in Babylon, the Israelites expressed their faith by imaging God also as their creator and their shepherd. The psalms reflect this evolution. The people's understanding of peace began from an initial conviction that peace was the fruit of God's saving work on behalf of the community; with that insight, peace was seen to extend also to the individual, to other nations, and to all creation. Peace took on the connotation of freedom from fear, a feeling of security and well-being founded on God's loving fidelity to the covenant as much as on God's mighty acts of liberation in Israel's history. The covenant which bound God and his people was understood to be a covenant of peace, unity, harmony, justice, and compassion to the poor. Although the political situation of harassment and oppression by pagan nations challenged the people's trust in the covenant of peace, the psalmists and prophets kept alive the vision of a future kingdom of peace, security, and quiet resting-places. "The Lord will bless his people with peace" (29:11). The Lord promised "peace on your borders" (147:14).

Peace in the positive sense of well-being, freedom to serve God in the covenant community, harmony with nature and with oneself, friendly relations with others—meanings implicit in *shalom*—was expected here and now in the present life, not in another world. The holy city of Jerusalem and the whole nation would experience an era of peace: "For the peace of Jerusalem pray: 'Peace be to your homes! May peace reign in your walls, in your palaces, peace!' " (122:6-7). Peace was a divine gift to pray for and be grateful for. It was expected that God would establish the kingdom of everlasting peace through an ideal king as described in Psalm 72. "In his days justice shall flourish and peace till the moon fails. ... For he shall save the poor when they cry and the needy who are helpless. He will have pity on the weak and save the lives of the poor" (72:7, 12-13).

Important to note is the close connection between peace and the works of justice, bringing relief to the oppressed. Psalm 72 realistically united them, even in poetic language: "May the mountains bring forth peace for the people and the hills, justice" (72:3). There will be no peace without justice for all, freedom for all. Justice taken in a narrow sense may not sufficiently transform and humanize society, for the height of justice can be the height of injury. The justice that makes peace possible is justice in the broad sense, including compassion, understanding, forgiveness, patience, love. The psalmist imagined justice and peace meeting and exchanging a kiss in greeting: "Justice and peace have embraced" (85:11). If all people are to enjoy peace and freedom, then all will have to put a hand to the task. Peace is not given to us ready made, but is a gift that has to be worked for, prepared for, struggled for, as well as prayed for. Only in this way will all "enjoy the fullness of peace" (37:11).

The psalms reflect a search for personal, inner peace as well as for the political peace and security of the entire community. Yahweh makes his covenant and speaks his word of peace to the community as a whole, but the individual is not an anonymous, interchangeable part of the whole. In the psalms, individuals sometimes emerge in their uniqueness to stand before God and receive God's word of peace in their inmost hearts. "I will hear what the Lord God has to say, a voice that speaks of peace, peace for his people and his friends and those who turn to him in their hearts" (85:9).

Inner peace, peace of heart, is possible for the individual even in the midst of affliction and of turmoil in the community. The secret lies in freely yielding to the will of God that gives meaning to the events of life. The psalms express this insight with the vocabulary of resting, being still, dwelling, turning to God in the heart. "In God alone is my soul at rest" (62:2, 6). In Babylon, the exiles eventually found some consolation as they sat in mourning, gazing at the flowing river: "By the rivers of Babylon there we sat and wept, remembering Zion" (137:1). The flowing river had a lesson to teach them about the futility of resisting God's plan to punish and purify and someday to restore his people. As they unlearned the ways of aggression, mastery, control, and grandiose achievement, they learned the ways of inner peace. Peace comes when we are willing to be still, patient, receptive, open, trusting, moving with the current of God's will that flows in stillness. "Be still and know that I am God, supreme among the nations, supreme on the earth" (46:11).

Nevertheless, the stillness of inner peace is not the stillness of a bump on a log. The psalmists had no praise for the torpor of apathy, but only for life and free choices. In the words of a modern psalm by poet T. S. Eliot:

> We must be still and still moving
> Into another intensity
> For a further union, a deeper communion.[11]

Inner stillness is the condition for deeper communion with the source of all freedom, and also the condition for the fruitful achievement of life's tasks. Peaceful people peacefully assume their responsibilities in the world, preparing peacefully for the future. "See the just man, mark the upright, for the peaceful man a future lies in store" (37:37).

Jubilant

We know from the slave songs of blacks in America before emancipation that religion can bring comfort and joy to the cheerless lives of enslaved people. All the more can religion be a source of joy to the free. The psalmists, who knew both oppression and freedom, were people who genuinely enjoyed God and enjoyed celebrating their religion in dance and song. The expressions of jubilation in the psalter are too numerous to be accidental occurrences or affected sentiments. The joy of the psalmists was genuine: the irrepressible outpouring of deeply grateful hearts.

The psalmists took their religion and their prayers seriously, as duties that demanded attention and fidelity, but they also took them playfully. The image that springs to mind in this context is that of King David "leaping and dancing before the Lord" with utter abandon as he and all the Israelites brought the ark of the Lord up to Jerusalem "with shouts of joy and to the sound of the horn" (2 Sam 6:15-16). Many of the psalms are attributed to King David, at least as their exemplar, and a spirit of celebration moves through the psalter. "I find my joy in the Lord" (104:34). "My heart and my soul ring out their joy to God, the living God" (84:3). For C. S. Lewis, this joyful spirit was the most endearing quality of the psalter. He wrote: "The most valuable thing the Psalms do for me is to express that same delight in God which made David dance."[12]

Genuine joyfulness and gaiety are infectious. Those nearby are soon caught up in the mood, unless they are neurotically gloomy. The psalmist urged others to share the abundant joy: "Let the hearts that seek the Lord rejoice" (105:3). "Ring out your joy to the Lord, O you just; for praise is fitting for loyal hearts" (33:1). With the enthusiasm of a cheerleader, the psalmist called on everyone to sing and make merry to the Lord: "All peoples, clap your hands, cry to God with shouts of joy!" (47:2). "Rejoice, rejoice in the Lord, exult, you just! O come, ring out your joy, all you upright of heart" (32:11). Nature herself was invited to join the merrymaking: "Let the heavens rejoice and earth be glad, let the sea and all within it thunder praise, let the land and all it bears rejoice, all the trees of the wood shout for joy" (96:11-12).

A primary motive for such unrestrained celebration was the experience of God's liberating, saving deeds. Set free from affliction, the psalmists rejoiced in the presence of God, their savior-liberator. "My soul shall be joyful in the Lord and rejoice in his salvation (35:9). "You have been my help; in the shadow of your wings I rejoice" (63:8). "You have made him rejoice with the joy of your presence" (21:7). There is no exhilaration like the total release from bondage, total liberation: "When the Lord delivered Zion from bondage, it seemed like a dream. Then was our mouth filled with laughter, on our lips there were songs" (126:1).

Even before the moment of liberation, the psalmists anticipated the joy that was to come and prayed for the consolation that would outweigh all the afflictions of the past (90:13). The psalmists' fond desire was to serve the Lord in freedom and gladness. They longed to participate once again in the festive gatherings in the temple on the great feastdays: "How I would lead the rejoicing crowd into the house of God, amid cries of gladness and thanksgiving, the throng wild with joy" (42:5). "I will come to the altar of God, the God of my joy" (43:4).

God was not the only source of joy in the psalmists' life. They were also quick to appreciate all the good things of life: feasting, dancing, the beauties of nature, the fruits of the earth, including "wine to cheer man's heart" (104:15). They delighted in song, poetry, and sometimes in the whimsical creations of imagination as when they pictured the mythological denizens of the deep sea, "and the monsters you made to play with" (104:26). The psalmists found particular joy in children, and were certain that children had a special place in God's affection too. "On the lips of children and of babes you have found praise to foil your enemy"

(8:3). "Truly sons are a gift from the Lord, a blessing, the fruit of the womb" (127:3). Fertility was an evident sign of a secure and happy future (128:3; 37:26). They prayed that Yahweh would always deal kindly with them "as a father has compassion on his sons" (103:13). People who can find joy in God in the midst of affliction, and joy in children, wine, and the beauties of nature are radically liberated people. They "serve the Lord with gladness" (100:21). Life is to be affirmed as it comes along, because life comes from God who made us for gladness and goodness.

When the psalmists attempted to put the joy of their heart into words, the favorite formula seemed to be "Blessed be God" (68:36). These brief syllables, or other phrases built on the verb "bless", are like a joyful explosion of praise, glory, adoration, gratitude. To bless is to give something in response to another, a way of returning thanks and good wishes, a way of honoring and complimenting someone. The psalmists lived in full awareness of God's blessings to them, and they were eager to make some response: "My soul, give thanks to the Lord; all my being, bless his holy name. My soul, give thanks to the Lord and never forget all his blessings" (103:1-2).

Many psalms celebrate the blessings of freedom, life, peace, prosperity, and fecundity of land that God has showered on his people. It is in accordance with God's nature to bless, to pour forth his goodness, and pile proof upon proof of his loving care for all creatures that his hands have made. "God, our God, has blessed us" (67:7). Blessing calls for blessing in return, even when the return must fall far short of being adequate. The heartfelt "Blessed be the Lord!" that the psalmists said back to God summed up everything they wanted to offer in gratitude and joy. Their blessing came from and expressed their whole being. The first and final words of Psalm 104 are identical—"Bless the Lord, my soul"—according to a poetic structure that neatly frames and responds to the enclosed verses enumerating God's blessings in creation. The name of God is often blessed in the psalms, because the name stands for the unnamed mystery that the psalmist honored: "I will bless your name forever; I will bless you day after day and praise your name forever" (145:1-2). In Psalm 135 we find an invitation to every class in the covenant community to join in a public, concelebrated blessing of God in the liturgy:

> Sons of Israel, bless the Lord!
>   Sons of Aaron, bless the Lord!
> Sons of Levi, bless the Lord!
>   You who fear him, bless the Lord!
> From Zion may the Lord be blessed,
>   he who dwells in Jerusalem! (135:19-20).

It was also customary to bless other people. The name or blessing of God was invoked in order to wish others well. Travelers who met on the road might greet each other with an exchange of blessings. A passerby might call out a blessing on those working in the fields, making sheaves from armfuls of grain: "On you the Lord's blessing! We bless you in the name of the Lord" (129:8). Not only by words of blessing, but by their presence, actions, and attitude, those who were themselves blessed became a benediction in the lives of everyone they encountered. People are sustained and helped to grow by the blessing they receive from others.

In their joy and gratefulness for the blessing of freedom, the psalmists had a perspective on the world that was more securely grounded than mere optimism. Their perspective joins that of the author of the first story of creation: "God looked at everything he had made, and he found it very good" (Gen 1:31). The world was primordially and irrevocably blessed when God gazed upon it and pronounced it good. To be aware, as the psalmists were, of having been blessed in innumerable ways is to live with a vision of the basic goodness of the universe, and to believe that God intends to make everything work together for his glory and the good of all he loves. The psalmists could affirm the radical goodness of life, nature, and history because they trusted the power of God's original blessing. "He remembers us, and he will bless us" (115:12).

Nobility and Frailty

Many psalmists, though not all, lived in a world they considered blessed in spite of everything. Their poetry expressed wonder at the beauty of the surrounding universe, fascination with the mysteries of nature, admiration at the countless forms of life and the uniqueness of humanity's role in the cosmos. They felt their own responsibility as stewards of God's creation with the obligation to manage, develop and direct things as best they could for the good of all. On every distant horizon they perceived the creating, liberating God.

Psalm 29, possibly influenced by Canaanite sources, is an exclamation at the power of Yahweh manifested in a thunderstorm: "The Lord's voice flashes flames of fire" (29:7). Psalm 104 enthusiastically celebrates the creative, ordering wisdom of God manifested in the heavens, on earth, and in the history of all living beings. The fertility of the land, the seasonal rains, the abundant wheat fields and pastures are attributed to God's loving care in Psalm 65. The word of God and his vivifying breath or spirit summon all things out of chaos into solid existence, according to the insight of Psalm 33: "By his word the heavens were made, by the breath of his mouth all the stars. . . . He spoke; and it came to be. He commanded; it sprang into being" (33:6, 9).

It was in this general context of God's mastery over all creatures that the psalmists reflected on their own being and their intimate relationship with God. They had no doubts that God himself made them, claimed them, knew them through and through, kept them constantly in his mind and cared for them. God knows his servants better than they know themselves, and no emotion or thought, no good or evil inclination, is hidden from the one who "knit me together in my mother's womb" (139:13). Psalm 139 reflected in awe upon the immensity and intimacy of the divine knowledge, and prayed that God might lead his servants along the path that ends in life eternal. In this way the psalmists made the reality of their own being and their personal history into a prayer glorifying the creator. They knew the uniqueness and originality of their position in the array of God's works—less than the heavenly beings but greater than cattle, sheep, and savage beasts (Psalm 8:6-9). They consented to their place, and willingly passed the glory on to God: "Not to us, Lord, not to us, but to your name give the glory" (115:1).

Although the psalmists were well acquainted with affliction and with their own personal limits and failings, they seem in general to have had a sense of the basic rightness of their human condition. They had a healthy self-image. We do not find them cursing the day of their birth as Job did (Job 3:3), or cynically mocking the vanity of all human effort as Qoheleth did (Eccl 2:23). In times of affliction they complained to God with all their might, but without acid recrimination and resentment over life itself. More frequently, we find acclamations of grateful wonder, and expressions of pride in their own potential: "I thank you for the wonder of my being, for the wonders of all your creation" (139:14). Appreciation of their own uniqueness and originality did not blind them to a realistic appraisal of their human frailty. They accepted human weakness without despairing of God's mercy. With no suggestion of boasting, they sang of being crowned with the glory and honor of God's image (8:6). Their favored status in God's plan and the freedom they enjoyed as Israelites were illustrations of the way God wished to act toward all.

The psalmists' understanding of human existence was limited by their confusion about the condition of human beings after death. The obscurity of this matter has not entirely disappeared several millennia after the psalmists, but today there is no longer a widespread belief in an underground abode of the dead called Sheol. Referring to Sheol, Psalm 115 said: "The dead shall not praise the Lord, or those who go down into the silence" (115:17). Sheol was a place of silence and darkness, "the land of oblivion" (88:13). Did all go to Sheol after death? The psalmists did not know for sure. Sheol seemed the appropriate place for the wicked, perhaps with supplementary "fire and brimstone" (11:6) to compensate for their self-indulgent life on earth. "This is the lot of those who trust in themselves, who have others at their beck and call. Like sheep they are driven to the grave, where death shall be their shepherd" (49:14-15). The just ones, who had experienced God's nearness and liberating power in this life, hoped for a better lot for themselves.

Some hoped they might escape death entirely, like Enoch and Elijah (116:8; 73:24-26). Others trusted that God would not let them decay in Sheol but would set them free and lead them to glory where he would show them his face and be their possession forever (86:13; 103:4; 49:16; 16:10). They compared death to falling asleep, and hoped they would awake to the fullness of joy forever: "As for me, in my justice I shall see your face and be filled, when I awake, with the sight of your glory" (17:15).

Happiness in the afterlife was not a certainty for the psalmists, but only a bright hope based on God's mercy.[13] If they served God and remained faithful to his covenant, it was not out of certainty of a future reward, not out of enlightened self-interest. What they knew for sure was that life is short and swift, and human beings are as fragile as the flower of the field (103:15). "Remember, Lord, the shortness of my life and how frail you have made the sons of men" (89:48). "Mortal man is no more than a breath" (39:12). "Our life is over like a sigh" (90:10). "My days are like a passing shadow and I wither away like the grass" (102:12). In such circumstances it is wisdom to seek values that are permanent, and especially to seek the favor of Yahweh, for "the love of the Lord is everlasting" (103:17).

Sinful

The wisdom to live as one should was as rare in the psalmists' day as in any period of history. Immediate, tangible realities are usually more influential on human behavior than considerations about immortality, future happiness, and the invisible creator of all that is seen. In spite of their giftedness and religious sensitivity, the psalmists were no strangers to moral failings. Those who exulted in being crowned with glory and honor, and holding power over the works of God's hands (8:6-7), were all too ready to "exchange the God who was their glory for the image of a bull that eats grass" (106:20). They fashioned idols and worshipped the work of their own hands. They used their freedom to declare independence and refuse to serve Yahweh. When punishment followed their sin, they repented and begged forgiveness. The psalmists experienced the human condition in its full range from degradation to exaltation. They acknowledged the shadow side of the human personality as well as the godly side.

Although the psalmists proposed justice and holiness as ideals, they had to live with the consequences of sinfulness in themselves and in society around them. There are passages that sound self-righteous and seem to point the finger of blame at others and even at God (44:18-22). Usually, however, the psalmists were openly contrite about their own failings. They took refuge in God's mercy, recalling how he had forgiven the sins of their fathers, and how he had pardoned King David for the murder of Uriah and for adultery with Bathsheba. Psalm 51, perhaps the finest prayer of repentance, carries an inscription attributing it to David "when Nathan the prophet went to him after his sin with Bathsheba" (51:2).

The psalmists were realistic enough not to expect total sinlessness even from themselves, but they expected sinners to "turn away from evil and do good" (37:27). The just may stumble but can rise again: "Though he stumble he shall never fall for the Lord holds him by the hand" (37:24). God himself cooperates in the recovery of a sinner by sending appropriate punishment, and then by removing both punishment and guilt when the sinner repents. "Now I have acknowledged my sins; my guilt I did not hide. I said: 'I will confess my offense to the Lord.' And you, Lord, have forgiven the guilt of my sins" (32:5). The desire to escape further punishment is the usual motive for repentance in the psalms, rather than pure sorrow for the offense given to God (40:13).

The sin denounced most frequently and vigorously in the psalter is idolatry. In the polemic against idols, the psalter is in the tradition of prophetic and deuteronomic writings of the same period. The first commandment of the Sinai covenant was the prohibition of idols (Dt 5:8). The psalter has its own version: "Let there be no foreign god among you, no worship of an alien god. I am the Lord your God" (81:10). The psalmists seemed to find some satisfaction in mocking and denouncing their idolatrous Canaanite neighbors, as if they themselves would never bow before Baal or eat offerings made to lifeless gods: "Let those who serve idols be ashamed, those who boast of their worthless gods" (97:7). Yet the Canaanite religion with its gods, myths, and fertility rites was a perennial source of temptation for the Israelites. Perennial was the call to turn away from idols and serve the living God.

A considerable level of risk seemed involved in serving the living God who permitted no carved images of himself and who remained an unknowable mystery even when he intervened in history on Israel's behalf. Yahweh remained out of grasp, out of control, beyond manipulation. Idolatry can be understood as a search for greater security from a thing over which one has some control. In the sixteenth century, John Calvin commented: "The human mind is an idol factory in constant operation." An idol—whether it be a wooden statue or something like fame, power, money, success, pleasure, national prestige—functions as a symbol of personal security, importance, immortality. For an idol, one is prepared to make any sacrifice and give all that is asked. From the viewpoint of the covenant with Yahweh, all idolatry is a kind of adultery. God responded to this insult like a wounded lover: "With their mountain shrines they angered him; made him jealous with the idols they served. God saw and was filled with fury; he utterly rejected Israel" (78:58-59).

The psalmists used the images of pictorial language to speak to God and about God, but images need not become idols. It was helpful to picture God in some mental image because a human being cannot easily approach or have a personal relationship with the totally unknown. For example, some psalms speak of seeking the face of God, though they do not attempt to describe facial features. A literary image of God is recognized as nothing more than an image, useful in speaking about what transcends human experience but infinitely inadequate to express the transcendent reality. A mental or verbal image becomes an idol when it is idealized and absolutized, equivalently carved in wood or stone, endowed with fervent expectations, and defended against challengers. Of these idols the psalmists said, "The gods of the heathens are naught" (96:5). When the nothingness of an idol is revealed, the idealized image collapses, and the worshipper's illusions along with it. The psalmists invited such a one to turn from disillusionment to the liberating God, acknowledging God's greatness and uncontrollable mystery. "He fixes the number of the stars; he calls each one by its name. Our Lord is great and almighty; his wisdom can never be measured" (147:4-5).

In the typical stages of the life-cycle, the mature years often bring an experience of disillusionment, a shattering of the idols that youth and naivete had erected. The world one has lived in comfortably enough and taken for granted over the years can be shattered by sudden loss, accident, or other forces beyond one's control. Without fully analyzing this experience, we may note that the painful moment of shattering may also be a moment of genuine freedom, including release from patterns of sin. At such times, if we listen to our own inner truth and deepest convictions, and to the word of God, our true self may emerge purified and strengthened. The crucial choice would be to live from now on in that experience of freedom, clinging no longer to a lost past, but centered on the present moment of possibility in which God sees and loves us as we are.

Conclusion

In this chapter we have listened to the psalmists speak for themselves about themselves. From their self-descriptions we can build up a composite portrait of one who is just before God, poor, afflicted yet serene with inner peace and joy, a person sometimes sinful but always ready to make a fresh beginning with God's help. Although this portrait is composed from the phrases of many different psalmists, we may see it as the description of a free man or woman, a person who stands before God and the world in the full religious, existential dimensions of human freedom. Furthermore, we recognize that according to the psalter a person is free because he or she has been set free by the divine liberator. "You called in distress and I saved you" (81:8). The following chapter focuses more directly on the liberating God.

Looking back over the characteristics of the free person, it becomes evident that the principal features appear in the gospel portrait of Jesus Christ. Jesus was that just one who, upon coming into the world, said: "Here am I. In the scroll of the book it stands written that I should do your will. My God I delight in your law in the depth of my heart" (40:8-9; Heb 10:5). Jesus was the poor one among the *anawim,* who extended an invitation to the world: "Take my yoke upon your shoulders and learn from me, for I am gentle and humble of heart" (Mt 11:29). From the depths of affliction on the cross, Jesus prayed in the words of Psalm 22: "My God, my God, why have you forsaken me? You are far from my plea and the cry of my distress" (22:2). On a still deeper level, Jesus preserved an unshakable inner peace and joy based on confidence in God's faithful, caring presence. "And so my heart rejoices, my soul is glad; even my body shall rest in safety. For you will not leave my soul among the dead, nor let your beloved know decay" (16:9-10). The confidence of Jesus was vindicated in his resurrection from death, when he emerged into a new existence of freedom and life-giving power: "The last Adam has become a life-giving spirit" (1 Cor 15:45). The final action of the risen Christ was to bless the disciples he left behind: "He led them out near Bethany, and with hands upraised, blessed them. As he blessed he left them, and was taken up to heaven" (Lk 24:50-51). All these significant aspects are familiar from the themes studied in this chapter. Jesus Christ is par excellence the free one profiled in the psalms. In a fourth-century commentary on the psalter, St. Hilary of Poitiers called faith in Christ the "key to the psalms" and said:

There is no doubt that what is said in the psalms should be understood according to what is preached in the gospel. . . . For in its entirety it is ordained to knowledge of our Lord Jesus Christ's coming, his incarnation, his passion, his kingdom, and his own and our glorious resurrection.[14]

NOTES

1. Albert Gelin, *The Psalms Are our Prayers,* trans. Michael Bell (Collegeville: Liturgical Press, 1964), p. 48.
2. The Hebrew word for ponder means to mutter or murmur under one's breath according to the oriental manner of assimilating religious texts. See: Is 8:19; 16:7; Jer 48:31; 1 Sm 1:12-13. "It is not the same as the Western way of meditation, which is interested in the contents of texts, studying them with the heart as well as with the intellect, but it is the repeated recollection of well known texts, looking for arbitrary associations while reciting and hearing the sound of the words. It is the activity of muttering, hearing and reading the sacred texts, by which the memory and the heart become full of the contents." H. J. Franken, *The Mystical Communion With JHWH In the Book of Psalms* (Leiden: E.J. Brill, 1954), p. 21.
3. C. S. Lewis, *Reflections on the Psalms* (New York: Harcourt, Brace & Co., 1958), p. 58.
4. Louis Bouyer, *The Meaning of Sacred Scripture,* trans. Mary Perkins Ryan (Notre Dame, Indiana: University of Notre Dame Press, 1958), p. 235.
5. Raymond Brown, *The Birth of the Messiah* (Garden City, New York: Doubleday, 1977), p. 351.
6. Albert Gelin, *The Poor of Yahweh,* trans. Kathryn Sullivan (Collegeville, Minnesota: Liturgical Press, 1964), p. 51.
7. Michael Gasnier, *The Psalms, School of Spirituality* (London: Challoner, 1962), p. 80.

8. For a development of this thought, see Simon Tugwell, *The Beatitudes* (Springfield, Illinois: Templegate, 1980), p. 44.

9. American theologian John E. Skinner has commented: "A part of being liberated from cultural oppression is precisely to see it not as a cross God wants the person to bear, but rather as a prefabricated illusory network developed by others who wish to keep certain people in their place; from the development of their powers; from the acceptance of their finiteness." *The Christian Disciple* (Lanham, Maryland: University Press of America, 1984), p. 46.

10. National Conference of Catholic Bishops, *The Challenge of Peace: God's Promise and Our Response* (Washington, D.C., 1983), pp. 10-13. Peace reaches its fullness of meaning in the mystery of Christ: "It is he who is our peace" (Eph 2:14).

11. T. S. Eliot, "Four Quartets: East Coker," in *The Complete Poems and Plays* (New York: Harcourt, Brace & World, 1971), p. 129.

12. C. S. Lewis, *Reflections on the Psalms* (New York: Harcourt, Brace and Co., 1958), p. 45.

13. There is no consensus among scholars about whether the psalmists believed in resurrection and immortality. The prevailing opinion has been that they did not, but I am following the opinion of Mitchell Dahood who identified some forty psalm texts implying belief in immortality and resurrection. Mitchell Dahood, *Psalms III* (Garden City, New York: Doubleday & Company, 1970), pp. XLI-LII.

14. Hilary of Poitiers, *Tractatus super Psalmos, Prologue* 5, in J. P. Migne, ed., *Patrologiae Cursus Completus* (Paris: Vrayet, 1844), vol. 9, col. 235, author's translation.

CHAPTER SIX

THE LIBERATING GOD

What does the psalter tell us about the liberating God? If the psalter is to be our school of prayer, the images of God that we find in it deserve close attention. They affect the way we understand and approach God in prayer. Theologically, prayer begins with the help of divine grace, but experientially it begins with the image of God that we hold consciously or preconsciously. If we were not convinced that there is a God worth praying to, we would direct our efforts elsewhere.

The psalmists had no doubts about the reality of the liberating God. They knew God as the one who brought Israel out of Egypt, "arm outstretched, with power in his hand, for his love endures forever" (136:11). It was this liberating God that they contemplated, reflecting more and more deeply on his saving works. The psalmists were not inclined to abstract speculation about the nature of God but were captivated by concrete images of God's presence based on their experience. As Thomas Merton observed:

> The contemplation we learn from the Psalter is not mere "speculation." The Psalms are not abstract treatises on the divine nature. In them we learn to know God not by analyzing various concepts of His divinity, but by praising and loving Him.[1]

In their songs of praise and love, the psalmists did not describe God as "the unmoved mover of all moving things," as Aristotle did. Aristotle's description is the conclusion of a process of logic. The psalmists were content with stating what might be the premises of that conclusion. Theirs was the language of poetry and prayer more than of rational logic.

Anthropomorphic Language

The psalmists did not philosophize about God, but they used language that was sometimes more concrete and at other times less concrete. In some psalms, God is called "rock." Elsewhere the psalmist says of God, "You neither change nor have an end" (102:28). Abstracting as we must in this chapter from the complex problem of the psalms' chronology, there is a progression of thought from the concrete to the universal. Both descriptions of God—as rock and as without change or end—express the same concept of permanence, but the language has changed. God imaged as a rock is closer to tangible, daily experience than the formless figure who never changes or has an end.

Progression from the visible to the invisible seems congruent with the usual modes of human thought and experience. It was in this evolving way that Israel came to know God more completely and that God revealed the mystery of his hidden face to Israel. The process was historical as well as theological, and was influenced by the changing political, intellectual, and cultural conditions of life among the people of God. This people experienced being liberated from Egyptian slavery under the leadership of Moses and Aaron by the power of "the God of Abraham, the God of Isaac, the God of Jacob" (Ex 3:15). They experienced God's care for them in the wilderness and his military brilliance in the conquest of Canaan. The memory of the psalmists dwelt upon those events and others during the period of the judges and kings, during the exile to Babylon, and the revival of Yahwism following the return to Jerusalem.

Israel's earliest images of God were drawn from the experience of historical events and from objects in nature associated with the saving, liberating action of Yahweh. Subsequent reflection on these images and experiences led to conceptual clarification. An appropriate language was elaborated. God who provided water from the rock and manna from the sky became known as the changeless, timeless, holy mystery who "does whatever he wills" (135:6). The liberating God who drew near to his people was also worshipped as the awe-inspiring king of glory: "I tremble before you in terror" (119:120). Anthropomorphic descriptions of God as a magnified human being were balanced by a reverence that dared speak only of God's holy name.

This chapter attempts to follow the shift or evolution in the psalter's images of God. The first group of images presented below seems to highlight God's nearness, while the second group focuses on God's transcendent mystery. This classification may be helpful, although it is partly arbitrary since some of the images overlap at the edges. No single image provides a totally adequate description, since the living God overlaps the edges of all our concepts. The two groups also complement one another and coexist in a necessary and meaningful tension. The liberating God exists in a freedom that escapes all limitations of human language. Commenting on the expressive value of images, theologian Kathleen Fischer notes: "The full significance of any individual metaphor for God can be understood only in relation to the complete range of Names for God."[2]

Images of Nearness

The aim of the psalmists was not to theologize about the existence and attributes of God but to call on God and rejoice in God: "My heart and my soul ring out their joy to God, the living God" (84:3). The existence of the living God was asserted without need for proof. His livingness is the source of life. Without God nothing lives: "You take back your spirit, they die, returning to the dust from which they came. You send forth your spirit, they are created" (104:29-30). Only evildoers behave as if there were no God: "The fool has said in his heart: 'There is no God above' " (14:1). Pagan nations have gods of their own, depicted in idols of silver and gold, but these are "false and empty gods" (31:7). The psalmist ridiculed the pagan idols: "They have mouths but they cannot speak; they have eyes but they cannot see" (115:5). Although the psalmists never doubted Yahweh's existence and supremacy above all idols and gods, time was needed before they unhesitatingly proclaimed: "You are great and do marvellous deeds, you who alone are God" (86:10).

Liberator. The living God of the psalmists is the one who acts on their behalf. More specifically, God is the one who delivered his people from bondage in Egypt, the savior and liberator of Israel. We recall that the notion of liberator is implicit in the Hebrew word for savior. "You are God my savior" (25:5). Because of this historical experience, Israel had a strong conviction of being a people chosen by Yahweh from the beginning of time to be his own special possession out of all the nations on earth. "He has not dealt thus with other nations; he has not taught them his decrees" (147:20). The decrees of the covenant linked Israel securely to the all-

directing will of God. Israel knew God as "Lord of salvation" who would never forsake his covenant partner (3:9).
God stands ready to repeat his act of liberation throughout
history for all who trust in his saving power. Liberation
from an external threat is usually envisioned, but sometimes
deliverance from sin is explicit: "Israel indeed he will
redeem from all its iniquity" (130:8). Dangers described as
exterior can also be metaphors for inner, spiritual affliction.
Sin is the universal source of evils. Yahweh is not a savior
because Israel is innocent and lovable but because Yahweh
is true to his word and merciful to those who need salvation.

Warrior. God's power to save was revealed to Israel when
he marched forth at the head of his people as their cham-
pion in battle (68:8). From his mighty deeds at the crossing
of the Reed Sea and in the conquest of the promised land,
Israel knew Yahweh as "the valiant in war, . . . the Lord of
armies" (24:8, 10). "O Lord God of hosts, who is your
equal? You are mighty, O Lord, and truth is your garment"
(89:9). Before the ark of the covenant found a final resting
place in the temple of Jerusalem, it was sometimes carried
on campaign with the army as a sign of Yahweh's presence
(see Jos 6:6; 2 Sm 11:11). The warrior-God was able to wield
the elements of nature as weapons aginst the enemy. "He
shot his arrows, scattered the foe, flashed his lightnings, and
put them to flight" (18:15). Psalm 18, which we have
already studied as a freedom-song, used vivid anthropomorphic imagery to depict the power and wrath of the warrior-
God who is master of wind and storms. "Smoke came forth
from his nostrils and scorching fire from his mouth. . . . The
foundations of the world were laid bare at the thunder of
your threat, O Lord, at the blast of the breath of your
anger" (18:9, 16). Earthquake and tornado obey the will of

the warrior-God: "He looks on the earth and it trembles; the mountains send forth smoke at his touch" (104:32). The uncontrolled power of nature is a sign of God's presence.

Companion. In the covenant agreement, God promised to be with his people forever, to liberate and rescue them. He promised to hear their cry for help and answer, "Here I am!" (Is 58:9). The psalmists had unlimited confidence in their divine companion: "The Lord is at my side; I do not fear. What can man do against me?" (118:6). "If I should walk in the valley of darkness, no evil would I fear; you are there" (23:4). So close is the Lord that he provides shade against the hot sun: "The Lord is your guard and your shade; at your right side he stands" (212:5). The image in Psalm 73 is of companions walking hand in hand: "I was always in your presence; you were holding me by my right hand" (73:23). The psalmists trusted that God was always with them even though weakness and frailty prevented them from always turning to the presence of God. Those who acknowledged their weakness and poverty could count on God's preferential nearness: "The Lord is close to the broken-hearted; those whose spirit is crushed he will save" (34:19). God did not restrict his companionship to those of high political or priestly rank but was present to all his people, especially the humble and poor.

Helper. God's presence with his people was not detached or indifferent but a befriending, helping presence. "The Lord is at my side as my helper" (118:7). He is "a helper close at hand in time of distress" (46:2). "You have been my help; do not abandon or forsake me, O God my help" (27:9). "The Lord is our help and our shield" (33:20; also 115:9, 10, 11). "I have God for my help" (54:6). The most immediate, spontaneous plea that the psalmists made to God in time of affliction was, "Help us" (79:9). The opening verse of Psalm 70 expanded this brief cry into a short prayer that was the favorite invocation of the early Christian monks and nuns in the deserts of Egypt. The verse is still used at the beginning of each liturgy of the hours: "O God, come to my assistance, O Lord make haste to help me" (70:2). As a helper and support to his people, Yahweh collaborates with them, acting in partnership to win their freedom. The Hebrew word that describes Yahweh as the psalmist's helper is the same word used by the author of the second creation story to describe the helper created to be Adam's partner (Gen 2:18, 20). The discovery of this female helper, so complementary and congenial to him, prompted Adam's cry of delight: "This one, at last, is bone of my bones and flesh of my flesh!" (Gen 2:23). The Psalmists echoed this exclamation in their prayers to Yahweh, their helper: "You console me and give me your help!" (86:17).

Compassionate. The psalmists knew that God could be angry with his people for their infidelities, but they trusted his compassion and mercy more than they feared his wrath. When God gave his commandments to Moses on Mount Sinai, he identified himself as "The Lord, the Lord, a merciful and gracious God, slow to anger and rich in kindness and fidelity" (Ex 34:6). This basic revelation of the divine nature was never forgotten. The psalmists loved to dwell on the compassion of God because they placed their hope in this steadfast attitude of God. "You, God of mercy and compassion, slow to anger, O Lord, abounding in love and truth" (86:15). "The Lord is kind and full of compassion, slow to anger, abounding in love" (145:8). Compassion draws God to interact with his people and take their burdens on himself.

The psalmists knew a God who was moved by the suffering of the poor and oppressed, as a loving parent is moved by the suffering of its child. They chose a parental image to convey the compassion of God: "As a father has compassion on his sons, the Lord has pity on those who fear him" (103:13). "Father of the orphan, defender of the widow, such is God in his holy place" (68:6). The psalmist felt "Your hand ever laid upon me" like a parent caressing, cherishing its child, comforting it by a gentle touch (139:5). The language used to image Yahweh is masculine; he is a father; but the imagery of compassion is also feminine and maternal. It might be said that God was considered to be asexual, for it was never permitted to depict Yahweh in any form, and no female divine consort for Yahweh was ever recognized. The masculine designations of God found throughout this book are not a statement about God's gender but the custom of common usage.

Good. "How good is the Lord to all, compassionate to all his creatures" (145:9). The goodness of God was often linked with compassion and mercy which manifest it: "Surely goodness and kindness shall follow me all the days of my life." (23:6). Once again, the psalmists' conviction resulted not from abstract calculation but from historical experience. As biblical theologian Xavier Leon-Dufour points out: "Having known evil in its greatest degree during the slavery in Egypt, Israel discovers good in Yahweh, her liberator."[3] Psalm 107 repeats a grateful response four times: "O give thanks to the Lord, for he is good" (107:1, 15,21, 31). Yahweh's name was called good (58:4), and Yahweh himself was called sweet and delightful: "Taste and see that the Lord is good" (34:9). The temple in Jerusalem was where the psalmist could most easily savor the goodness

of God: "We are filled with the goodness of your house, of
your holy temple" (65:5). Worshippers were swept away by
the beauty of the temple's architecture and liturgical services, and they equated God's radiant beauty with his ineffable goodness. The goodness of God that they experienced
in the temple was only a foretaste of the goodness prepared
for them by God in the land of the living: "I am sure I shall
see the Lord's goodness in the land of the living" (27:14).
"How great is the goodness, Lord, that you keep for those
who fear you" (31:20).

Provider. Yahweh's great goodness was the source of all
blessings in the life of his people. Psalm 103 praised God as
the universal provider "who fills your life with good things"
(103:5). Not only spiritual blessings of forgiveness and peace
came from Yahweh, but the necessities of daily life: "The
Lord is compassion and love; he gives food to those who
fear him" (111:4-5). The role of nurturing life as a loving
provider emphasizes a feminine quality of God. In several
picturesque passages the psalmists reflected on the way God
provided food even for wild beasts, birds, and fish
(104:10-28; 147:9). "The eyes of all creatures look to you
and you give them their food in due time. You open wide
your hand, grant the desires of all who live" (145:15-16).
The earth itself is enveloped in God's gentle care with appropriate allotments of sunshine, rain, snow, and wind.

If Yahweh's providence shows predilection for any
creatures, it is for those who depend entirely upon him
because they have no resources of their own. "It is he who
gives bread to the hungry, the Lord, who sets prisoners free,
the Lord who gives sight to the blind, who raises up those
who are bowed down, the Lord, who protects the stranger
and upholds the widow and orphan" (146:7-9). There is no

one who is not precious and deserving of care from God the provider. The psalmist had the boldness to pray, "Guard me as the apple of your eye" (17:8). As one protects one's eyes and allows nothing to touch the pupil of the eye, so the psalmist trusted in God's care. God's watchful protection lasts day and night, since God never tires: "No, he sleeps not nor slumbers, Israel's guard" (212:4).

Shepherd. The image of a shepherd protecting and providing for the needs of the flock was a familiar sight in rural Israel. In addition, there was the abiding memory of the forty-year journey through the desert: "He brought forth his people like sheep; he guided his flock in the desert. He led them safely with nothing to fear" (78:52). Moses who had been shepherd for Jethro was Yahweh's representative: "You guided your people like a flock by the hand of Moses and Aaron" (77:21). In their prayers, the psalmists were persistent in reminding God that he was their shepherd and they were the flock that had to be led by his hand (95:7; 100:3; 28:9). "O shepherd of Israel, hear us, you who lead Joseph's flock" (80:1).

Psalm 23, beginning "The Lord is my shepherd," has always been one of the most loved and commented psalms in the psalter. For many who have learned it by heart or sung it, Psalm 23 has provided comfort "in the valley of darkness" (23:4). The psalmists found the image of a shepherd an unforgettable expression of God's nearness to his people. When affliction struck them, they appealed to this image in their prayers for divine forgiveness and mercy: "Why, O God, have you cast us off forever? Why blaze with anger at the sheep of your pasture?" (74:1; 44:12, 23).

Healer. Every generation shares the human experience of sickness, but each age has its own view of the causes and cures of particular diseases. According to the religious mentality of the psalmists, sickness was caused by sin, and God was the healer. Although the word for healer does not occur in the psalter, as it does in Ex 15:26, the notion is expressed in equivalent terms: "The Lord will help him on his bed of pain, he will bring him back from sickness to health" (41:4). "O Lord, I cried to you for help and you, my God, have healed me" (30:3). The psalmists were keenly aware of their mortality, especially when compared to God's everlasting life (39:6, 12; 102:24). Several psalms have been called "the psalms of the sick" (Psalms 6, 38, 41, 102). These contain first-hand descriptions of sighs, groans, racking pain, anguish and sleepless nights. Clinical diagnoses are not given, but we recognize the common, universal symptoms of advanced illness: "I have reached the end of my strength" (88:5). Besides physical problems, the sick sometimes had to confront social rejection and gloating enemies (38:12; 41:8-9). In their affliction, the sick turned to God the healer, usually coupling their prayer with an expression of contrition for sin. In Psalm 107, we find a succinct description of the process in which the liberating God healed his servants:

> Some were sick on account of their sins
> and afflicted on account of their guilt.
> They had a loathing for every food;
> they came close to the gates of death.
> Then they cried to the Lord in their need
> and he rescued them from their distress.
> He sent forth his word to heal them
> and saved their life from the grave. (107:17-20)

Personal Name. God was given many titles such as healer or shepherd, but the personal name of God had to be revealed by himself. Moses had asked God's name at the theophany in the burning bush, and God revealed himself as Yahweh, the God of Abraham, Isaac and Jacob. When Moses pressed for further clarification, he was given the mysterious assertion, "I am who am" (Ex 3:14). Some of the numerous interpretations of this name find in it a promise of God's abiding presence in the world. Martin Buber commented:

> YHVH is "He who will be present" or "He who is here," He who is present here; not merely some time and some where but in every now and in every here. Now the name expresses His character and assures the faithful of the richly protective presence of their Lord.[4]

The psalmists invoked God's personal name—usually translated "Lord"—with great frequency and familiarity. His name brought them gladness and strength, for it summoned his presence to them. It was for this reason that God told his people his name. Theologian Walther Eichrodt has said, "By revealing his Name God has, as it were, made himself over to to them; he has opened to them a part of his very being and given them a means of access to himself."[5] The pagan nations showed their scorn for Israel's God by mocking his name: "How long, O God, is the enemy to scoff? Is the foe to insult your name forever?" (74:10). The psalmists erased the insults by their extravagant praise: "Praise the name of the Lord. ... Lord, your name stands forever, unforgotten from age to age" (135:1, 13).

As reverence for God's personal name increased, it was pronounced less frequently. Instead of saying "the name of the Lord [Yahweh]", the psalmists said "your name," "his name," or used a different designation. This custom, which originated to safeguard God's honor, tended to make God more remote. A subtle distance is felt between God and a psalmist who talks about "the name" instead of saying "Yahweh." The affection, joy, and saving power that had been associated with "Yahweh" were transferred to "his name." "O God, save me by your name; by your power, uphold my cause" (54:3). What was lost in familiarity was gained in respect, as the psalmists directed their prayers to an unnamable God.

Rock. When God is imaged by impersonal metaphors, we are reminded that our notion of a human person is not fully adequate to the divine reality. Among the impersonal images of God in the psalter—such as shield (7:11), sun (84:12; cf. 57:12), lamp (18:29), winged bird (36:8)—perhaps one of the most disconcerting to modern ears comes in verses that say, "Who is a rock but our God?" (18:32). Since we find this metaphor more than half a dozen times, it is not easy to ignore it totally. Its use in the psalter is only part of a more extensive tradition in the Old Testament, which is not without its influence on New Testament patterns of speech. In addition to literary usage, there are indications, in Israel's history, of stone columns or pillars erected as symbolic reminders of Yahweh (Ex 24:4; Is 19:19). The patriarch Jacob seemed particularly fond of these standing stones (Gen 28; 31; 35). Stone pillars were frequently used by the idolatrous worshippers of Baal.

When the psalmists called Yahweh their rock, they were evoking an image that conveys unfailing reliability. God is the solid bedrock where one can always touch home and begin building again. As a commentator explains:

> What is implied in calling Yahweh "rock" "crag" or "stone" is reference to his role as the sure support and pro-

tector of his people—i.e. as a rock provides the foundation and material for solid building, shade from the scorching summer sun, and a hiding place for the guerrilla fighter.[6]

A further meaning is implicit when the psalmist says, "You are my father, my God, the rock who saves me" (89:27). The association of rock with God's fatherhood suggests that God's features are engrained in his children as if his offspring had been hewn from him as from a quarry (Dt 32:18; Is 51:1).

The poetic climax of the Book of Job alludes to God's action as laying the cornerstone of the earth (Job 38:6). Later Jewish commentators described this cornerstone as the navel of the earth, the original point from which all dry land extended over the primordial waters. It was from this bedrock, supposedly, that the temple of Jerusalem rose to a peak like a mountain.[7] The psalmists saluted the holy mountain where God made his dwelling, "Mount Zion, true pole of the earth" (48:3).

Sanctuary. The sanctuary of the temple in Jerusalem was the innermost room, the holy of holies. The sanctuary was not identified with God, but was the place where his presence was concentrated, his earthly dwelling or resting place among his people. "I gaze on you in the sanctuary to see your strength and your glory" (63:3). "The Lord has chosen Zion; he has desired it for his dwelling: 'This is my resting-place forever, here have I chosen to live" (132:13-14). The psalmists loved to stand in the courtyard of the temple and raise their hearts and hands to God in prayer: "I lift up my hands in prayer to your holy place" (28:2; 134:2). "How lovely is your dwelling place, Lord, God of hosts! My soul is longing and yearning, is yearning for the courts of the Lord" (84:2-3). It was the presence of

Yahweh in the sanctuary that drew the psalmists on pilgrimage three times a year. "O Lord, I love the house where you dwell, the place where your glory abides" (26:8). With an envious eye on those who always lived near God in the sanctuary, the author of Psalm 27 made this prayer: "There is one thing I ask of the Lord, for this I long, to live in the house of the Lord all the days of my life, to savor the sweetness of the Lord, to behold his temple" (27:4).

Inside the sanctuary was the ark of the covenant containing the two stone tablets of the law. On the lid of this covenant box were mounted two winged figures called cherubim. Psalm 80 begs God's help, saying, "Shine forth from your cherubim throne" (80:2). The wings of the cherubim formed God's throne so that he rested his feet on the lid of the covenant box as on a footstool, claiming and protecting it. "Let us go to the place of his dwelling; let us go to kneel at his footstool" (132:7). The ark disappeared during the destruction of the temple and the city by Nebuchadnezzar in 586 B.C. In the second temple, built after the return from exile in Babylon, the altar of holocausts assumed some of the significance formerly attached to the ark as the specific area of God's presence.

Eventually this temple too was destroyed by invaders. With the repeated destruction of material sanctuaries, the Israelites remembered that God had promised to be with the *people* as his primary abode, and that he chose a place for the sake of the people not vice versa (2 Mc 5:19). One of the psalmists recalled: "When Israel came forth from Egypt, ... Judah became the Lord's temple, Israel became his kingdom" (114:2). Yahweh could be approached in the altar, the covenant box, the temple, the city of Jerusalem, and the promised land itself at one time or another, but could always be found present with his people as a whole.

Images of Separateness

We have found in the psalms numerous images of familiarity with God, "for what great nation is there that has gods so close to it as the Lord, our God, is to us whenever we call upon him?" (Dt 4:7). Images of nearness have their counterpart in images of separation. The Hebrew verb "to separate" is the root of the word for "holy." The holy God is by nature wholly other and separate from everything profane or unclean. Some images of God, such as king or creator, have a strong basis in concrete materiality even as they convey notions of separateness. Other images and descriptions in the psalms convey God's otherness indirectly, by emphasizing the psalmist's feelings and reactions to the liberating God. God who liberates his servants is himself sovereignly free and untameable. The psalmists never attempted to domesticate God. The images to be explored in this section show how the psalmists safeguarded God's holiness even while they experienced his nearness.

Holy. Holiness is attributed to God as freely as misdeeds are attributed to human beings. An aura of holiness surrounds the psalmists' image of God, enveloping the divine with ineffable mystery and inaccessibility. "Let them praise his name, so terrible and great; he is holy, full of power" (99:3). The holy is felt to be "full of power," a power that may break forth against the unholy at any moment without warning. God's moral perfection demands that all who approach him cleanse themselves from all that is unholy, sinful. God's holiness calls not only for freedom from sin but also for ritual purity, freedom from anything thought to be unclean and displeasing to Yahweh. Worshippers offered sacrifices for sin and bathed to remove ritual impurity. "To prove my innocence I wash my hands and take my place around your altar" (26:2). "O purify me, then I shall be clean" (51:9).

Several times the psalmists called God "the Holy One of Israel" (71:22; 78:41; 89:19) without providing a more detailed description of God enthroned in majesty, such as we find in Isaiah or Ezekiel. The psalmists knew that God's ways are holy, and that he is the living source of all holiness, but his holiness remained an impenetrable mystery in itself. The Holy One of Israel is utterly unlike the gods of other nations with their predictable, human-sounding histories of strife and passion. A god found to be just like ourselves would be no god worth worshipping. The Holy One of Israel throning in the temple was adored as holy mystery. "I bow down before your holy temple, filled with awe" (5:8). God's holiness is a numinous quality, not readily captured in rational concepts. Rudolph Otto, the author of a classic study of numinous phenomena, noted how incomprehensible and mysterious is the holy, "how, incalculable and 'wholly other', it mocks at all conceiving but can yet stir the mind to its depths, fascinate and overbrim the heart."[8]

King. Originally a tribal confederacy acknowledging an unseen God as their only king, Israel became a monarchy under Saul, David, Solomon and their successors. The psalmists had personal experience of kings and the customs of kingship. Their national king was the highest authority in the land, combining functions of judge, general, priest, sage, and ceremonial figurehead. To the commoner, the king surrounded by his courtiers was a remote and splendid personage; even King David's own son Absolom "fell on his face to the ground before the king" to do him homage (2 Sm 14:33). When the psalmists wished to stress the sovereignty of Yahweh, the image of king was at hand. "The Lord is king!" shouts the author of Psalm 97 in the opening verse. The psalm speaks both of earthly kings and of God as king; prerogatives of the former may be attributed to the latter and vice versa, by reciprocal influence. Earthly and heavenly elements coalesced in the image of an ideal, messianic king whom all nations would serve: "It is I who have set up my king on Zion, my holy mountain" (2:6).

Several psalms have been called "enthronement psalms" because some modern scholars infer the celebration of a New Year's festival in Jerusalem enthroning Yahweh as king of Israel (especially Psalms 47, 93, 96-99). Another group, called "royal psalms" (Psalms 2, 18, 20, 21, 45, 72, 101, 110, 132), praises or prays for the earthly king who rules as Yahweh's delegate. From all these psalms we can learn that the function of kings, whether human or divine, was not primarily to be served and waited upon but to serve the people by ruling wisely and mercifully. The king assured his people of the blessing of peace and liberty. It was he who was expected to uphold the widow and orphan, protect the stranger, raise up those who are bowed down, crush the oppressor, "save the poor when they cry and the needy who are helpless" (72:12). The king would make justice flourish by helping, healing, guiding, and correcting his people. "In splendor and state, ride on in triumph for the cause of truth and goodness and right" (45:4).

For their part, the people responded to their king, whether human or divine, with devout homage. They sang praise to their king with all their skill, crying out with shouts of joy (47:2, 8). They prayed that his kingship stretch to the ends of the earth and last forever (98:3). To the king's presence they brought their offerings, bowing low in worship (96:8). A personal relationship of loving surrender becomes problematic when the king is approached only with elaborate ceremony. In this way, the distance between the king and his faithful subjects increased. The reigning divine king was described in language that grew more and more exalted: "The Lord is king, with majesty enrobed; the Lord has robed himself with might, he has girded himself with power" (93:1). The king was exalted far, far away.

Glory. The majesty of the divine king radiates in a shining, shimmering, spiritual substance called glory. In itself, glory is the radiance or reflection of God's holy majesty. The psalmists associated glory with light, which is the most brilliant but intangible of created realities: "Lord God, how great you are, clothed in majesty and glory, wrapped in light as in a robe" (104:1-2). The sun, moon, and stars are brilliant, but they proclaim a greater brilliance: "The heavens proclaim the glory of God" (19:1). The psalmists were dazzled by the divine splendor, for "the Lord is glorious on high" (93:4).

The final section of Psalm 24 is a dialogue about the coming "king of glory." According to Hebrew usage, "king of glory" is probably equivalent to "glorious king." In the psalm, a command is given to the city gates to "lift high your heads, grow higher, ancient doors" in order that the glorious king might enter (24:7). The gatekeepers ask for identification, "Who is the king of glory?" (24:8). The question gives the psalmist an opportunity to honor Yahweh with splendid titles, calling him "the mighty," "the valiant"—"He, the Lord of armies, he is the king of glory" (24:10). The dialogue is repeated once more in slightly different form; the psalm is a successful poetic attempt to honor God by praising his glory.

To honor God is thought to add to his glory in some way. The psalmists spoke of glorifying God, or giving God glory, by their words of acclaim and by their deeds. "Glorify the Lord with me, together let us praise his name!" (34:4). "Not to us, Lord, not to us, but to your name give the glory" (115:1). Yahweh deserves to be glorified by people of every nation: "Give the Lord, you families of peoples, give the Lord glory and power, give the Lord the glory of his name" (96:7-8). In his turn, God gives his faithful servant a share in his own glory. "He will give us his favor and glory" (84:12). The saving deeds of the liberating God culminate in the glorification of his servant: "I will save him in distress and give him glory" (91:15). The more God's glory abounds, the closer the world comes to the goal envisioned by the psalmist, when "his glory fills the earth" (72:19). On that future day, in the temple of the whole world, "they all cry: 'Glory!' " (29:10).

Creator. Reflection on Yahweh's kingship and his saving, liberating deeds may have led the Israelites to a conviction that "the Lord does whatever he wills, in heaven , on earth, in the seas" (135:6). The liberation-event of the exodus was a new creation of the people of God. God acts towards all of nature and all nations as if all belonged to him. "The Lord's is the earth and its fullness, the world and all its peoples" (24:1). The king of glory claims sovereignty over all, and his claim is based on the most radical assertion possible—Yahweh is the original source of all that is.

The Canaanites, Babylonians and other cultures that interacted with Israel each had their own mythology about the origin of the world. These myths often described a primordial struggle between the gods and the forces of chaos. Traces of cultural influence from these myths may be detected in psalms that speak of trampling Rahab underfoot (89:11), and crushing Leviathan's heads (74:14). Other references to the raging, foaming ocean or river may also be allusions to the power of the mythical, watery chaos. According to the psalter, however, the forces of nature were not pre-existing antagonists conquered by Yahweh but creatures shaped by his hand and subject to his word of command. "He commanded: they were made" (148:5).

Nothing pre-existed Yahweh, for he is the author of all that is, "the maker of heaven and earth" (115:15). The creator was understood to be eternal. He never came to be; instead, he is the one to whom it can be said, "From all eternity, O Lord, you are" (93:2). Compared to human beings whose days of life are like a fading flower, "you are God, without beginning or end" (90:2). Heaven and earth themselves are transitory compared to the eternal creator: "They will all wear out like a garment. You will change them like clothes that are changed. But you neither change nor have an end" (102:27-28). Just as the creator has no beginning, neither can the psalmist imagine him ever coming to an end. "You, O Lord, will endure forever" (102:12).

The creator who endures forever is the goal towards which all creation is oriented, in the psalmists' view. The author of Psalm 148 called on sun and moon, sea creatures and oceans, mountains and hills, beasts wild and tame, young men and maidens to praise the name of Yahweh; the whole cosmos was summoned to acknowledge that it exists for Yahweh. The people of God, his faithful servants, acknowledge that they do indeed belong to Yahweh, their creator, and depend entirely on him to give final meaning to their lives: "Know that he, the Lord, is God; he made us, we belong to him" (100:3). The psalmist's relationship with

God as creator is one of gratitude and respectful wonder; the creator's power and wisdom are too overwhelming to invite a relationship of casual familiarity. The creator knows all the psalmists' actions and writes them in his book (139:16). There are no secrets hidden from the one whose hands shaped the hearts of all people and who calls each star by name (119:73; 147:4; 33:6). The psalmist knelt in homage and amazement before such wisdom (95:6). "It was you who created my being, knit me together in my mother's womb. I thank you for the wonder of my being, for the wonders of all your creation" (139:13-14).

Psalm 104 is outstanding among the psalms that celebrate Yahweh as creator. Walther Eichrodt has commented on the psalm's idyllic description of nature: "Its picture of the world is completely filled with the idea of the unity, the coherence, the harmonious order of the cosmos."[9] God's plan assigned each creature its proper place and appropriate activity for the mutual benefit of all. The psalmists depicted a cooperative interdependence and kinship of creatures among themselves, all existing in co-dependence on the one creator. We might expect to find evidence of the psalmists' concern with domestic and agricultural matters such as rain, crops, cattle, but their appreciation of nature extended to a universal fellowship. Wild goats, storks and the birds of heaven, sea monsters, lions and all the beasts of the forest, living things great and small—God feeds them all in due season as he feeds his people with bread, oil, and "wine to cheer man's heart" (104:15). Mountains and hills, meadows and valleys, deserts and oceans, eagerly await the divine creative breath that renews the face of the earth (104:30).

Scholars have found resemblances between Psalm 104 and a fourteenth century B.C., Egyptian Hymn to Aton, the sun god. In the psalms we find traces of a cosmology or view of the universe that may contain some elements commonly held in the ancient Near East along with other elements unique to Israel's faith in Yahweh. The universe was thought to be constructed in three stories. On the lowest level were the waters of chaos. The middle story consisted of the earth, with Sheol somewhere in its depths. The psalter does not address the technical problems involved in stabilizing the land-mass upon the abyss of waters, except to attribute the feat to Yahweh. "It is he who set it on the seas; on the waters he made it firm" (24:2; cf 104:5; 96:10).[10] Arching over the earth was the third story called the firmament or vault of heaven. This is the sky with its visible sun, moon, and stars. To account for precipitation, there was water above the firmament (148:4) that could be let down at Yahweh's command through windows or gates in the sky. "He commanded the clouds above and opened the gates of heaven" (78:23).

Where does Yahweh dwell? Psalm 2 says he "sits in the heavens" (2:4). His throne was placed far above the turmoil of earth, with a commanding view of all his creation: "He stoops from the heights to look down, to look down upon heaven and earth" (113:6). Other psalms located God's dwelling precisely in a balcony above the waters of heaven: "Above the rains you build your dwelling" (104:3). God thrones in the heaven of heaven, the highest heaven, in a position of unrivalled preeminence. All honor belongs to the creator "who alone made heaven and earth" (146:6). Creation was the first of the saving, liberating acts of the Lord Most High.

Most High. In this title we have the culmination of the psalmists' efforts to exalt God by situating him high above the realm of ordinary human life. The title refers not only to Yahweh's throne above the heavens, but also to his moral perfection and his kingdom of glory (113:4). All things lie at the disposal of the Most High, for "the Lord does whatever he wills" (135:6; 115:3). To God in the highest belongs the right to assign a specific task or goal to all creatures: "It is he, the Lord Most High, who gives each his place" (87:5). His name is "the Lord, the Most High over all the earth" (83:19). The title is not an original expression but was appropriated from a deity in the Canaanite pantheon (see Gen 14:18-20). By the time of the psalmists, the Israelites were well aware that "God the Most High" was their redeemer (78:35). The title occurs frequently in the psalter.

The Most High was not pictured as reigning in solitude. As befitted so exalted a monarch, a vast court of ministers surrounded him and waited upon him. These heavenly ministers made up the divine assembly. The psalmists occasionally called these courtiers gods, but more often angels. "God stands in the divine assembly. In the midst of the gods he gives judgment" (82:1). Without a doubt Yahweh surpassed all these spirits in dignity and authority, for he was the Most High. "You indeed are the Lord Most High above all the earth, exalted far above all spirits" (97:9). The heavenly spirits exist to praise the Most High, carry his messages, protect his servants on earth (91:11; 148:2; 104:4). "Give thanks to the Lord, all his angels, mighty in power, fulfilling his word, who heed the voice of his word" (103:20). In battle, the Most High could call on hosts of angels to spread fury, rage, and havoc, "a troop of destroying angels" (78:49).

For people with wicked designs, the remoteness of the Most High was an invitation to transgress with impunity.

"They say: 'How can God know? Does the Most High take any notice?' " (73:11). On the journey to the promised land, the rebellious Israelites "defied the Most High in the desert" (78:11). For the pious psalmists, however, the thought of the Most High was inspiration to sing psalms, make music, and rejoice (9:3; 92:2). The Most High could inspire fear as well as joy in the hearts of those who appreciated the majestic sublimity of God. The power of the Most High to save and shelter his faithful was awe-inspiring even to those who benefitted from it. The psalmists stood in reverence before the Most High: "For the Lord, the Most High, we must fear, great king over all the earth" (47:3).

God as Most High is incomprehensible and immense. In the presence of the Most High, a believer becomes conscious of his or her creaturehood, a feeling of littleness and dependence before the numinous. Before the Most High, no one makes claims or boasts of strength. This creature-feeling has been well described by theologian P. van Imschoot: "Faced with the numinous, man has a strong sense of his own nothingness, shudders, is dumbfounded, and feels a reverential awe made up of terror, admiration and trust."[11] Before the Most High, the whole earth trembles because God surpasses all that the cosmos can contain and recognize as its own (104:32). The Most High is totally other, totally beyond reach, yet he knows the secrets of the heart (44:22). St. John Chrysostom in the fourth century was able to intuit the mentality of the psalmists when he wrote:

> When the psalmist gazes down into the immeasurable, yawning depth of divine wisdom, dizziness comes upon him and he recoils in terrified wonder and cries: "Too wonderful for me, this knowledge, too high, beyond my reach."[12]

The psalmists' lively sense of God as Most High kept them firmly established in humility and filial fear. Exhortations to fear the Lord are not uncommon. "Come, acknowledge the power of God. His glory is on Israel; his might is in the skies. God is to be feared in his holy place" (68:35-36). "O blessed are those who fear the Lord and walk in his ways" (128:1).

Conclusion

This chapter has distinguished two divergent views of the liberating God which can be found in the psalter. On the one hand there is the figure of the Most High, inaccessible and majestic, who caused the psalmist to say, "I tremble before you in terror" (119:120). This same liberating God could be described in images of nearness and tenderness that made another psalmist say, "To be near God is my happiness" (73:28). Images of nearness and images of distance co-exist in the psalter without difficulty. Sometimes they co-exist in the same verse, with no feeling of contradiction, as when a psalmist says, "The Lord of hosts is with us" (46:4), or "God the Most High [is] their redeemer" (78:35). The tension between nearness and otherness creates a more adequate image of the mystery of God than a one-sided stress on either aspect. What the psalmists believed about the liberating God found expression in images that are complementary, not contradictory, while the full picture inevitably falls short of the total truth about God. "My whole being will say, Lord, who is like you?" (35:10).

What we learn from the psalmists about the liberating God is precious in spite of its limitations (and we have not discussed all the psalter's imagery). We learn that the world and all its events and people form the arena of God's action and loving concern, while at the same time God stands sovereignly free in respect to all creation. The good shepherd who comforts his flock is the great king over all the earth. We learn also that the liberating God liberates without hesitation or regret, for he is not jealous of his peoples' freedom. God's own freedom surpasses human freedom in such a way as to encompass whatever use or abuse might be made of this gift. God saves by liberating and liberates by saving. We learn that God does not spurn a humbled, contrite heart, but promises that those who fear him need fear no evil. The psalmists' fear of God was balanced by a universal trust: "In him my heart trusts" (28:7). A love that was greater than fear gave them the certainty of being protected and cared for in every circumstance by the liberating God: "My hope is in you, O Lord" (25:21).

NOTES

1. Thomas Merton, *Praying the Psalms* (Collegeville, Minnesota: Liturgical Press, 1956), pp. 7-8.
2. Kathleen Fischer, *The Inner Rainbow* (Ramsey, New Jersey: Paulist Press, 1983), p. 111.
3. Xavier Leon-Dufour, *Dictionary of Biblical Theology,* 2nd rev. ed. (New York: Seabury Press, 1973), p. 214.
4. Martin Buber, *On the Bible* (New York: Schocken Books, 1982), p. 60.
5. Walther Eichrodt, *Theology of the Old Testament,* trans. J. A. Baker (Vol. 1, London: SCM Press, 1961), p. 207.
6. Norman K. Gottwald, *The Tribes of Yahweh* (Maryknoll, New York: Orbis, 1979), p. 684.

7. *Theological Dictionary of the New Testament,* trans. and ed. Geoffrey W. Bromiley (Vol VI, Grand Rapids, Michigan: Wm. B. Eerdmans, 1968), p. 96.

8. Rudolph Otto, *The Ideal of the Holy,* trans. John Harvey (New York: Oxford University Press, 1958), p. 80.

9. Walther Eichrodt, *Theology of the Old Testament,* trans. J. A. Baker (Vol. 2, Philadelphia: Westminster Press, 1967), p. 113.

10. Professor Bernhard Anderson of Princeton has commented that the three-storied universe is a religious statement rather than a technological or scientific theory. "In the psalms this language is used religiously or poetically to express the awareness that on all sides the historical world is threatened by powers of chaos which, were they not held back by the Creator, would engulf the earth and reduce existence to meaningless confusion." Bernard W. Anderson, *Out of The Depths: The Psalms Speak For Us Today,* rev. and enl. ed. (Philadelphia: Westminster Press, 1983), p. 124.

11. P. van Imschoot, "La Vie Spirituelle," 1946, quoted by Albert Gelin, *Key Concepts of the Old Testament,* trans. George Lamb (Glen Rock, New Jersey: Paulist Press, 1963), p. 27.

12. St. John Chrysostom, *On the Incomprehensible,* translated and quoted by Rudolph Otto, *The Idea of the Holy,* trans. John Harvey (New York: Oxford University Press, 1958), p. 182 quoting Ps 139:6.

CHAPTER SEVEN

FREE FOR A NEW LIFE OF LOVE

Deep prayer is a liberating experience. This concluding chapter brings together the experience of freedom and the attitude of prayer. In previous chapters we have explored separately the structure or qualities of freedom and prayer in the psalter, the profile of the liberated psalmist who prays, and the liberating God who is encountered in prayer. We have not yet seen how growth in prayer correlates with growth in personal freedom.

The correlation is not immediately evident if we understand freedom as the possibility of doing whatever we please, and prayer as total surrender to the good pleasure of God. The psalter, however, has shown us that true freedom is experienced when God liberates those who have placed all their hope in him. God's liberation begins with interior purification from the bondage of sin, and radiates out to ever-increasing horizons of personal, interpersonal, and sometimes political freedom. The psalmist who cries out for liberation from the snares of his enemies and then is miraculously delivered by divine intervention is celebrating in poetic language an experience of liberation that extends from the interior to the exterior.

The psalmist is set free by a God who shows love and who invites a response of trusting love in return. As justice and peace embrace, in the intuition of Psalm 85:11, so do freedom and prayer. They embrace in love and trust: in loving trust or trusting love. The psalter will unveil for us the reciprocal interaction between love and trust, prayer and freedom. Prayer implies trust in God's love, and this trust is liberating. To be free is to be able to love God; sometimes only this degree of freedom is left to an individual. Prayer frees us for a life of trusting love, and freedom opens new possibilities of praying, loving, trusting.

The first section of this chapter focuses on the theme of love as found in the psalter. The second section highlights attitudes of trust in the response of love. The psalmists were surprisingly expressive on both these subjects.

Love Without End

The Hebrew language has several terms for love, and these were used at least fifty times in the psalter. The psalmists spoke ten times more often of God's love for them than of their own love for God, but both attitudes are clearly present. The frequency of the language of love in the psalter alone would be enough to challenge the exaggerated view that the God of the Old Testament is a figure remote from human warmth and tenderness, inspiring only fear and trembling. God revealed in the Old Testament is the father of the Lord Jesus in the New Testament, and this "God is love" (1 Jn 4:8). The Old and New Testaments, taken in their totality, each present a balanced revelation of God's loving and awe-inspiring aspects. The New Testament, however, has a more advanced development of the ethical implications of the love of God, including love of all people, even enemies.

What do the psalmists understand by love? To modern ears, love often carries connotations of emotional and even romantic feeling that is not at all primary in the psalter, though not entirely absent either. For the psalmists, love is a comprehensive term for the bonding that holds a relationship together on conscious, preconscious, functional, and transcendent levels. Perhaps the primary expression of love between God and his people is action. On God's part, lovingkindness is expressed in liberating acts; the exodus from Egypt is recalled again and again as archetypal. On the psalmists' part, love for God is expressed in acts of thanks, worship, and fidelity to covenant obligations. "I have not hidden your love and your truth from the great assembly" (40:11).

The relationship of love between God and his people is a dialogue in which the first speaker is God. "It is the Lord who grants favors to those whom he loves" (4:4). The priority of God's love is evidence of its utter gratuity. Nothing the psalmist has done, but only the greatness of God's love, permits access to his presence in the temple: "I through the greatness of your love have access to your house" (5:8). God's love spells salvation; God sets free because of his love: "He brought me forth into freedom, he saved me because he loved me" (18:20).

The priority of God's love is not lessened because he acts in response to the psalmist's prayer. It is precisely to that gratuitous love and not to any other consideration that the psalmist's prayer appeals: "Stand up and come to our help! Redeem us because of your love" (44:27). "In the morning, fill us with your love" (90:14). The appeal to God can be on behalf of a single individual as well as the entire community. God's covenant of love with the people in general applies to each individual in his or her uniqueness. "O Lord, remember me out of the love you have for your people" (106:4). "In your love remember me" (25:7). "Let your face shine on your servant. Save me in your love" (31:17).

In some texts, God's liberating love seems to be conditional on the good behavior of the psalmist. The psalmist must hate evil, hold God in fear, or at least call upon God in prayer before God will show himself forgiving and full of love (Ps 66:20; 86:5; 97:10; 103:11). It is true that God does repay each according to his or her deeds (62:13), but God does not withhold his everlasting love from anyone. Even those who reject God's love or do not attempt to deserve it remain included in the greatness of a love that does not depend on their being lovable. This unfathomable divine love is partly frustrated and held in check by those who refuse to respond to it, but never abandons them entirely and is always available as the basis for reconciliation and conversion.

Yahweh keeps on loving faithfully forever. As Israel's covenant partner, Yahweh makes these promises of loyalty in Psalm 89: "I will keep my love for him always; with him my covenant shall last. ... I will never take back my love; my truth shall never fail" (89:29, 34). In return, the psalmist overflows with gratitude: "I thank you for your faithfulness and love which excel all we ever knew of you" (138:2). The first four verses of Psalm 11 give thanks to Yahweh by repeating the refrain, "His love endures forever," and Psalm 136 repeats the same refrain after each half verse for twenty-six verses. Yahweh's faithful love is celebrated in psalm after psalm. "Strong is his love for us; he is faithful forever" (117:2). "Indeed, how good is the Lord, eternal his merciful love" (100:5). "Your love, O Lord, is eternal, discard not the work of your hands" (138:8). "So I will give you thanks on the lyre for your faithful love, my God" (71:22). The author of Psalm 89 promises to match the eternity of God's love with an eternity of praise and song: "I will sing forever of your love, O Lord; through all ages my mouth will proclaim your truth. Of this I am sure, that your love lasts forever, that your truth is firmly established as the heavens" (89:2-3).

Whenever a psalmist had personal experience of God's tender, liberating love, the typical response was an exclamation of incredulous joy. "Blessed be the Lord who has shown me the wonders of his love" (31:22). "O Lord, how precious is your love ... Your love, Lord, reaches to heaven; your truth to the skies" (36:8, 6). "As for me, I will sing of your strength and each morning acclaim your love" (59:17). "For your love to me has been great" (86:13).

With this response we come to the second component of the dialogue of love between God and his people. The first word of love was spoken by God, but the beloved's reply comes next. Sometimes the reply is explicit, in the form of words that try to match God's own lovingkindness. "I love you, Lord, my strength, my rock, my fortress, my savior" (18:2). "I love the Lord for he has heard the cry of my appeal" (116:1). Sometimes the psalmist exhorts others to join these expressions of love. "Sing psalms to the Lord, you who love him" (30:5). "Love the Lord, all you saints" (31:24). "Sing a psalm to his name for he is loving" (135:3). The psalmist's response is more implicit when it takes the form of waiting for God's love (147:11), and never doubting the care of "the God who shows me love" (59:11, 18). To love God is life itself for the psalmist, or even better than life: " Your love is better than life, my lips will speak your praise" (63:4).

The psalmist's free response to God's love results in deep, mutual bonding: "You are loving with those who love you" (18:26). In a spirit of oneness with God, the psalmist was conscious of clinging to God and being held fast by God's right hand (63:3). God looks with love upon those who place all their hope in his love (33:18, 22). The psalmist wished to prolong the mutuality and intimacy of this experience: "Keep on loving those who know you" (36:11).

The psalmists' love for God extended to God's name, God's commands, God's temple, and all that belongs to God. All that God loves, the psalmists tried to love. God's love is universal, for "he fills the earth with his love" (33:5). Especially included in this universal love are the poor and lowly who have no one else but God to care for them. References in the psalter to the poor and afflicted may be considered expressions of the psalmists' love for neighbor as a corollary of love for God. The psalms do not attain the New Testament's lofty directives about love of neighbor and love of enemy. Instead, the Lord's enemies and the psalmist's enemies are unequivocally cursed. At the same time, we find in the psalms statements about the all-encompassing love of God that may surpass the author's own understanding of their meaning. There are echoes of universality in verses like the following: "O Lord, you are good and forgiving, full of love to all who call" (86:5). There are hints of the interdependence of all God's creatures in Psalms 104 and 148.

The psalms' character as love-poems can be appreciated best, perhaps, by someone who is in love. He or she would be sensitive to the many ways love can be expressed without using the word love. Psalm 42, for example, is the cry of someone yearning for God like a deer thirsting for running streams. There is the vehemence and passion of love in the words, "When can I enter and see the face of God?" (42:3). Psalm 73 casts a sidelong glance at the prosperity of evildoers, how sound and sleek their bodies are, but the author concludes that no created reality can compare with the bliss of loving Yahweh. "Apart from you I want nothing on earth" (73:25). Another psalmist felt held by Yahweh's tender hand and exclaimed, "My soul clings to you" (63:9), as wife to husband, using the same verb found in Gen 2:24 to describe marriage. Psalm 45 is a wedding song, somewhat like the *Song of Songs,* which can be applied to the psalmist's love for God the king. Like two lovers enthralled with each other's beauty, Psalm 45 breathes promises of intimacy and delights. "Listen, O daughter, give ear to my words: forget your own people and your father's house. So will the king desire your beauty: he is your lord, pay homage to him" (45:11-12).

The relationship of mutual love was a transforming influence in the life of the psalmists. The amiability of God prompted the psalmists to embrace God's will in its totality, loving what God willed in their life, in the lives of others around, and in the plan of history. Such love brings incredible peace and joy to the depths of the heart in spite of adversities and afflictions that make life difficult in many ways. The psalmists discovered how liberating God's love is, and how it delivers from anxiety and defensiveness. "Since he clings to me in love, I will free him" (91:14). Purified by the experience of loving and being loved by God, the psalmists had little fear of life or death. Only one thing mattered above all: "To be near God is my happiness" (73:28). Human personhood is not perfected except through liberating love. By love the psalmists climbed the mountain of the Lord and won the right to stand in God's holy place (24:3).[1]

Trust Without Fear

The centuries during which the psalms were composed were not continually peaceful and untroubled, any more than our own period of history when the world lives under the constant threat of universal nuclear destruction. Existence is always precarious and problematic, at least for a large percentage of people. Many psalms reflect the anxieties of the common people held in conditions of economic or political insecurity and unfreedom. The message repeated in numerous ways in the psalter is that God loves and cares for his people in spite of everything.

Affirmations of divine concern such as we have surveyed in the previous section are the foundation of trust. "In God I trust, I shall not fear; what can mortal man do to me?" (56:5). Trust is born in a climate of love and protectiveness. Human beings need repeated reassurance, affirmation, and promises before we begin to relax our modes of defensiveness and begin to trust the basic goodness of life. We need to be loved first, before feeling liberated enough to love and trust in return. One who has personally experienced Yahweh's benevolent power and presence can say: "Hope in him, hold firm and take heart, hope in the Lord" (27:14). Hope may be taken as synonymous with trust for the purpose of these reflections, although they are different terms in Hebrew. The psalms sometimes use the words in poetic parallelism: "It is you, O Lord, who are my hope, my trust, O Lord, since my youth" (71:5).

Those like the psalmists who have experienced themselves as cherished by God tend to be satisfied with nothing but that love and nothing other than that love. They tend to put their trust totally in the experience of being loved and loving

in return, which is the basic dynamic of the act of prayer.
Love simplifies their life and gives unifying meaning to its
events and activities. We call their attitude trust, in the sense
of turning confidently to Yahweh and drawing strength
from him in every situation of anxiety. "O my Strength, it is
you to whom I turn, for you, O God, are my stronghold, the
God who shows me love" (59:18).

Trust is based also on God's past reliability and
faithfulness to his word. When the psalmists were hard-
pressed, they turned to the all-powerful liberator who
delivered his people from the land of Egypt and cared for
them for forty years in the desert. The exodus and other
mighty deeds of Yahweh were not considered as past events
of ancient history but as experiences that lived on in the
community's faith and liturgical worship.[2] The past was
reactivated in the today of Israel's encounter with Yahweh:
"O that today you would listen to his voice" (85:7).

Confident reliance was nourished by Yahweh's saving
deeds in the psalmist's personal past history. "It is you, O
Lord, who are my hope, my trust, O Lord, since my youth.
On you I have leaned from my birth, from my mother's
womb you have been my help. My hope has always been in
you" (71:5-6). In times of battle, whether the battlefield was
literal or metaphorical, the psalmist had not put his trust in
chariot and horse, nor in his skill with bow and sword, but
trusted "in the name of the Lord" (20:8; 44:7). From past
experience he learned this truth: "He who trusts in the
Lord, loving mercy surrounds him" (32:10). "Those who
put their trust in the Lord are like Mount Zion, that cannot
be shaken, that stands forever" (125:1). The source of confidence is not God plus human resources, but God alone, as
Psalm 62 stressed by repeating "alone" five times in thir-
teen verses.

The psalmists lived with the sincere belief that all comes from God, and that they could entrust themselves to God's hands because all would work out according to his benevolent designs. In prayer and daily practice, they could turn over all their concerns to the one who was more concerned about them than they could be about themselves. "Entrust your cares to the Lord and he will support you" (55:23). "When cares increase in my heart, your consolation calms my soul" (94:19). Trust involves letting go of subtle and overt efforts to manipulate in order to remain in apparent control and apparent security. Trust has to do with relaxing one's desperate grip on life, so as to move with increased openness, acceptance, surrender, freedom.[3] The psalmists learned to trust Yahweh "at all times" (62:9), because "all his works are to be trusted" (33:4). Such trust is itself an experience of liberation that opens up a new space for living. Led by the shepherding staff of Yahweh, the psalmists found their way out of dark valleys to broad, green pastures where they lacked for nothing (Psalm 23).[4]

Trust in Yahweh casts out fear, but the psalmists did not live in illusions about the dangers they faced from enemies and other evils. Trust does not cast out risk, but counts the risk acceptable because of the trusted protector. "Since he is at my right hand, I shall stand firm" (16:8). There are some passages in the psalter where the poetic language about confidence in God's protection would be naive presumption if taken literally. For example, Psalm 91 (quoted in the New Testament by the tempter of Christ in the desert to elicit presumption—Lk 4:10) says there is nothing to fear from flying arrows, lions, vipers, and the wicked who seek to destroy. Usually, the psalmists were realistic about the dangers they faced, both interior and exterior. Their trust was great enough to see God's loving care in both the ups and downs of life.

The greatest danger that challenged the psalmists' trust was the approach of death. Death is the paramount day of evil and time of distress, especially when the question of life after death is still obscure. In good times, the psalmists could write breezy assurances that the Lord looks on "those who hope in his love to rescue their souls from death" (33:18). However, when the world that one has taken for granted collapses, and one is looking defeat and death in the eye, and the liberating God seems to be asleep or to have rejected his servants (44:10-26), then one's trust is put to the final test. The author of Psalm 31 felt "like a dead man, forgotten" (31:13), with fear and slander all around him. His spirit of trust remained indomitable. "As for me, I trust in the Lord: let me be glad and rejoice in your love. ... I trust in you, Lord, I say, 'You are my God.' ... Be strong, let your heart take courage, all who hope in the Lord" (31:8, 15, 25). A verse of this psalm was on the lips of Jesus as he died on the cross, according to Luke's gospel: "Into your hands I commend my spirit" (Lk 23:46; Ps 31:6). Elsewhere, the psalmist's final prayer seems to express confidence that death will bring blissful communion with Yahweh: "I am sure I shall see the Lord's goodness in the land of the living. Hope in him, hold firm and take heart" (27:13-14).

Loving trust in God is a strong and courageous attitude, even in the face of death, but it remains a highly vulnerable stance, dependent on divine support. "In you rests all my hope" (39:8). As an image of ultimate trust, the author of Psalm 131 evoked the picture of a child resting in its mother's arms. The child rests quietly, without anxiety, sustained by a lived awareness of being safe from all harm.

"Truly I have set my soul in silence and peace; a weaned child on its mother's breast, even so is my soul" (131:2). There is vulnerability in this posture, yet at the same time total security because of God's love. The psalmist was childlike, but not infantile, towards the divine maternal figure.

If we recall that the attitude of loving trust speaks to the psalmist's life of prayer, we see how these images evoke the deepest levels of prayer as a quiet resting in God. "Be still before the Lord and wait in patience" (37:7). Elsewhere, the psalmist returned to the theme of resting, with contemplative wonderment and praise, in the mystery of God's loving presence. "In God alone be at rest, my soul; for my hope comes from him" (62:6). It was St. Augustine, at the beginning of the second book of his *Confessions,* who gave classic formulation to the restless human search for a security and freedom that can never be touched: "You have made us for yourself, and our hearts are restless until they find their rest in you." The psalmists knew where their hearts should rest, and as often as they strayed from that sacred center they called themselves back: "Turn back, my soul to your rest, for the Lord has been good" (116:7). Prayer was their constant turning to the Lord, trusting totally in his faithful love, finding the meaning of life in his wisdom and transcendent goodness. "I trust in the goodness of God forever and ever" (52:10).

Conclusion

By exploring the themes of trust and love, we have touched the living attitudes that make the psalter a school of deep, liberating prayer. It is by appropriating these attitudes in our personal situation that we learn the ways of prayer,

under the guidance of the Spirit of freedom who dwells with
the children of God. Monastic author Thomas Merton expressed this opinion about the psalter:

> If, as the fathers tell us, this pure and ecstatic love for God,
> which flows from a knowledge of God as he is in himself, is
> the secret of contemplation, and if the Psalms are everywhere
> full of this love, then it is clear that the Psalter is a school of
> contemplation which has no equal except the Gospels and St.
> Paul.[5]

Aggressive people who are looking for quick results and
are achievement-oriented in their approach to prayer will
not find the psalter to be a handbook for the degrees of
prayer or for liberation movements. The psalter does not
present itself as a text for do-it-yourselfers. It teaches no
methods for liberating ourselves or becoming prayerful in
several, easy steps. Freedom and prayer come from beyond
ourselves; they are gifts rather than controllable experiences
that we can achieve by our own efforts. They are what the
power of God achieves in us when we are willing to be
trusting, patient, receptive, open, and unprogrammed.

The psalter is recommended reading for people who have
made the ego-shattering discovery that they are somehow in
bondage and unable to do anything about it. The psalms are
the prayers of ordinary people longing for freedom in every
sense of the word, but especially in the ground of their own
being where they are aware of God and of who they most
deeply are. As the desire for freedom grows stronger, the
psalter can direct us to the true source of freedom. The
psalms sketch the parameters of a new life of love, trust,
and freedom. Prayer is the breath of such a life.

Prayer and freedom are interconnected at their roots.
Both rise from the realization that we are called to live not in

the bondage of self-centeredness but in mutual, loving relationship with God and others. Renouncing manipulation, we discover freedom. We are not the self-sufficient, self-righteous center of the universe, but creatures made in God's image and likeness for a life of inner freedom and exterior collaboration. "Know that he, the Lord, is God. He made us, we belong to him" (100:3).

We belong, directly yet interdependently, to one who not only made us but who continues to be present to us with constant, loving care. To live that truth is to be free. To celebrate that truth is to pray. To experience that truth's full range of meaning implies total transformation of life. Here is the secret of the psalmists' inspiration, the wellspring of these songs of freedom. Transformed and liberated ourselves, we may join the psalmists in their new song of praise. "Let me sing to the Lord for his goodness to me, singing psalms to the name of the Lord, the Most High! (13:6).

NOTES

1. For a commentary on "the mountain of the Lord" understood as the highest degree of love, when one "no longer even loves himself except for God," see St. Bernard of Clairvaux, *On Loving God,* trans. Robert Walton, Cistercian Fathers Series 13 (Spencer, Massachusetts: Cistercian Publications, 1973), x:27.

2. "The act of deliverance, so to speak, remains active and potent throughout the continuing history of the people for whom it was wrought; in the biblical view it is not a mere event of the past, but something that is ever and again made present and real in the lives of those who celebrate it in word, and sacrament: the salvation that was once-for-all wrought for the whole people is appropriated by each family or each individual as the family or the individual makes response in worship and thanksgiving." *The Interpreter's Dictionary of the Bible* (Nashville: Abingdon Press, 1962), s.v. "Salvation," by Alan Richardson.

3. See the development of these notions in Carolyn Gratton, "Some Aspects of the Lived Experience of Interpersonal Trust," *Humanitas* IX:3, pp. 273-296. Also of special interest in this issue of *Humanitas* (November, 1973) devoted to the theme of Social and Interpersonal Trust are the articles by George W. Morgan (pp. 237-251) and Burkart Holzner (pp. 333-345).

4. For a fine commentary on Psalm 23 emphasizing the theme of trust, see Bernhard W. Anderson, *Out of the Depths,* rev. and enl. ed. (Philadelphia: Westminster Press, 1983), pp. 206-212.

5. Thomas Merton, *Bread In the Wilderness* (New York: New Directions, 1953), p. 107.